MEMOR
UNUSUAL AB   ..AN ON
RUSSIAN AND EAST COAST CONVOYS
IN WORLD WAR TWO

with my good wishes

David Cothell

MEMORIES OF AN UNUSUAL ABLE SEAMAN ON RUSSIAN AND EAST COAST CONVOYS IN WORLD WAR TWO

by

DAVID COTTRELL

The Memoir Club

First published in 2006 by
The Memoir Club
Stanhope Old Hall
Stanhope
Weardale
County Durham

British Library Cataloguing in
Publication Data.
A catalogue record for this book
is available from the
British Library

ISBN: 1 84104 141 6

Typeset by TW Typesetting, Plymouth, Devon
Printed by Antony Rowe Ltd, Eastbourne

Contents

List of illustrations

Dedication

To my friends and relatives who did not return from World War II and whom I never forget on Remembrance Day, and also my wife for her unfailing support for my yachting and boating activities since the war.

Foreword

The Rt Hon. the Lord Strathcona and Mount Royal

David Cottrell was indeed an unusual able seaman: distinguished by an adventurous spirit and perseverance (my family motto). He and I were both fortunate enough to have been given a good start in life – now over eighty years ago. Though our roots lie in different parts of the country – his in Gloucestershire whilst mine are in a remote island off the west coast of Scotland – we also share a common thread in a lifelong interest in ships and the sea, boats and water, where he has made a memorable public contribution. His grandfather's yacht sounds grander than anything my family ever had. He has led a varied and colourful life. Perhaps he has been lucky: but I suspect that he has a well-developed ability to spot an opportunity and go for it.

After public school and university – briefly in my case – we both joined the Navy and were sent to HMS *Ganges* across the water from Harwich. Like him, I remember the deplorable food; though public schoolboys were well inured to this, unlike many of our fellows. However, I go further: I remember it as the only time in my life in which I have been genuinely hungry. Young men undergoing energetic training which included an hour's rowing at dawn in naval cutters considered one slice of bread and one rasher of bacon to be short rations and complained vociferously. I have always suspected that there was something amiss in the administration. Nevertheless, the services have always been outstanding at training and rose to the wartime challenge for which there had been such a lamentable lack of preparation. For example, the less athletic among us, including me, all fell about laughing when the instructors demonstrated the test that we would have to pass. Yet twelve weeks later all but two out of a class of seventy went through the routine without problems.

His memories of the sick bay are happier than mine: though mercifully I was spared first-hand experience, my impression from

colleagues was of a brutal regime based upon the assumption that
those who reported sick were malingerers. It did little to change
my mind when, a year later, as a young officer first lieutenant of a
small Motor Torpedo Boat, based at Felixstowe across the water,
we had difficulty persuading *Ganges* staff to allow us alongside to
get treatment for a badly wounded sailor from our flotilla-leader's
boat which had been sunk in an action off the Dutch coast. It is
intriguing that in those days we may well have been on the same
anti-E boat patrols as *Puffin*.

Like him, I recall the pleasure of meeting the very agreeable
'Duggie' Graham at the Lancing section of the King Alfred officers'
training course; though I reckoned that he was a better naval padre
than he had been an Eton master. I sympathize with David in
finding the morse code (recently superseded) something of a
challenge; however I managed to struggle through and passed for
a commission. Whereas he had to wait for his technical bent to be
exploited as an electrical officer working on the primitive
equipment which we then called RDF.

David's description of life as a public schoolboy on the lower
deck demonstrates his good sense of humour and capacity to make
friends, often in uncomfortable circumstances.

After the war he went from strength to strength in the world of
recreational boating. It was there that our paths crossed again when
I brought my Silver motor boat up to Beechams' yard, where they
made an outstanding job of refurbishing it after a near disaster
entering Milford Haven in a gale. I often wished that I had a
boatyard to do proper jobs on my children's dinghies instead of my
clumsy efforts. His successes in saving and restoring canals in
Gloucestershire and imaginative efforts to improve coastal facilities
for yachtsmen are a lasting tribute to his determination when
roused.

Though it may be a far cry from his grandfather's 800 ton yacht,
I have a pleasant picture in my mind as the artist and his family
putter in their narrow boat along a beautiful canal which he has
the satisfaction of having saved for future generations – though
perhaps the rigours of an able seaman on a wartime Arctic convoy
will doubtless never be entirely forgotten.

Preface

The title of this set of memoirs indicates that the author must have done something or many things of an unusual nature in his lifetime, and that he went to sea as well. Both of these notions are correct in the case of David Cottrell who not only ran away from Eton College Windsor to go to sea, but also proved his desire to serve in the Royal Navy by volunteering for service in it during the Second World War, and served as an Able Seaman for three years at least before accepting any form of promotion. The story surrounding these facts has something of a unique quality, let alone adventure, and includes his experiences whilst on the now famous wartime Arctic convoys to Russia, and also includes many interesting experiences he encountered thereafter.

In fact the author has only set out to record some of these things as several people have more recently suggested that the connection between his disappearance from Eton College, and subsequent reinstatement there, and the wartime service in the Royal Navy on Russian Convoy, would be a fairly unique story to relate. Added to this is his experience as a yachtsman after the war, culminating in his election to the Royal Yacht Squadron in 1970, as probably the only Able Seaman member of that establishment, the preserve of many senior Naval Officers in addition to the ordinary members until then. Also after serving as a solicitor for twenty years his subsequent involvement in the marina industry and his leadership of that industry for a time, before his retirement and taking up practice as a landscape artist, conclude a fascinating story.

CHAPTER 1

Origin and early life

DAVID VERNON SWYNFEN COTTRELL WAS BORN on the 15th day of November 1923 and brought up at Bredon in the County of Worcester. My early upbringing took place in a privileged style in the Manor House of that village. My father, who was a solicitor in Birmingham, married when he came back from the First World War in 1918, and although my parents continued to live there for several years whilst they house hunted, they purchased the Manor House, Bredon, Worcestershire in 1921. My mother having been brought up in the countryside did not enjoy city life! My father then had to travel to his office in Birmingham every day by train, which as Bredon had a railway station in those days was very convenient. I shall be disclosing more of my father's background later on.

My mother, Dorothy Mary Catherine Cottrell (née Liddell) was born on 1 April 1896 in Peking in China, the eldest daughter of Captain C.O. Liddell who at that time lived in China as he had a trading company there. She married my father soon after the end of the First World War when he returned from service in the Army.

I believe that I am not alone in having very hazy recollections of my years before I could walk, but two things stand out, one being that my pram was often wheeled down to the builder's yard as my Nanny was a great friend of Mr Walter Wilkes the village builder, and secondly that my pram, when I was put out in the sun, was closely guarded by our Black Labrador named Tinker, whose face frequently came over the side of the pram to see if I was all right, and if so to give me a kiss. I have a brother, John, who is three years older than me, and his presence, and later on that of his governess, were a great influence on my early life. My parents had three staff living in as well so we were well looked after.

Before going to Prep School in 1931 I was well taught by two good governesses in the basics which are so important at an early

The Author (on the left) and some friends aboard HMS Kent *in 1942*

age. My mother who was an artist had also given me the basic approach to drawing, particularly perspective, which is so easy if taught at that age.

So it was that I was sent to boarding school at Arden House, Henley in Arden, which had just been handed to Mr J.P. Nelson as Headmaster by his father Dr Nelson. Like most of us there I immediately became homesick, but soon got over it. And so for the next few years I enjoyed life as far as one can at school, and the education subsequently proved to be good as I managed to pass the Common Entrance Exam into Eton in 1936.

In 1928 my Grandfather Liddell came to live with us for a time at Bredon after the death of my Grandmother and handed over his house at Chepstow to his eldest son. Hence we used to go with our governess and parents on board his yacht *Narcissus* for many of our holidays, including Cowes Week. She was 222ft overall, 816 tons, and very luxurious, and the interior is described in Maldwin Drummond's book *Saltwater Palaces*.

I mention this because my love of the sea started at that time, and that coupled with my friendship with another boy at Arden House School, Dennis Foster, were the important factors that were to shape a large part of my life certainly during World War II. Dennis Foster was good at mathematics like me, which was necessary to get into Dartmouth where he went after Arden House School, and being a friend he persuaded me to try and go there as well, particularly as I had spent quite a lot of time at sea in the yacht *Narcissus*. By that time we had not only been round Britain in her, but also out in the Mediterranean and to Lisbon and to Gibraltar, and I enjoyed being at sea.

I have mentioned before the good prep school education that I had at Arden House School, and it is interesting to record at this point that in May this year 2002, after I had started writing this account of my experiences, one of the old boys of that school, Michael Farrell, put on a reunion lunch for about seventy of us nearby. We all seemed to confirm our thankfulness for having such a good grounding in the classics, and maths in particular. In addition my mother being an artist had taught me perspective before I went to school, thus when I got there the Headmaster, the Late Jack Nelson, who was also Head of Art and a very good artist, took me under his wing. Another old boy who is a little older than me, Ian Jenkin OBE, was due to be present but could not come due to a last minute family commitment, and I remember him also having extra art lessons like me from Jack Nelson. So after the reunion I got in touch with him, as I had not seen him for some fifty years. I shall be referring to this towards the end of this book.

In mentioning the soundness of the grounding in education that I had along with my elder brother to start with, I must not fail to pay tribute to the governesses we had before we went to prep school. The earliest part of any education in my experience is what matters most, and after the age of eleven years it is more a case of enlarging knowledge.

And so it was that I was sent to Eton College Windsor as a new boy in the Summer Half of 1936, having passed the Common Entrance Exam well and achieved the Upper Fourth Form. I had a comfortable house at 'Westbury' in the Dorneywick Road, the Housemaster being Mr C.E. Sladden, a very nice man. I quite liked it there, though having been in the first eleven at cricket at Arden House School, I found the cricket at Eton exceptionally boring,

Narcissus, *R.Y.S. 1928*

more nets than playing! However this was not the point, I still longed to go to Dartmouth and to sea in the Royal Navy, which I felt would be much more to my liking as a future than life ashore. I again requested my parents once more during the summer holiday to let me be transferred, to no avail.

During the long summer holiday I considered what I might do as I had heard that it was possible to enter the Navy via the Merchant service; wishful thinking perhaps! I therefore conceived a plan to run away to sea if I had enough pocket money at the beginning of term to buy the necessary railway tickets to do so. I made it clear to my parents that I needed some more pocket money for my second term, and so I was provided with sufficient for what I had in mind to do, which was to travel to Tilbury Docks. Charlie Trapp, our chauffeur, who was a really nice ex-soldier of the First World War, duly delivered me back to Eton. I got the house porter to take my luggage to my room, and immediately made my way up to Windsor GWR station where I took a train up to London and thence to Tilbury, arriving there in the afternoon.

Why Tilbury, you might ask. This was because one summer, when my parents and I were on Grandfather's yacht *Narcissus* in the Mediterranean, we took passage back to the UK on the P&O liner *Viceroy of India*, and had been impressed by the young officers on board, who told me that it was a very good company to serve at sea in.

Needless to say due to my age, which of course I disclosed, they would not offer to apprentice me and told me to reapply after the age of sixteen. So it was that I had to retrace my footsteps back to London on the first train, and thence to Paddington Station. I then considered my position and concluded that it was no good going back to Eton as that would be the end of any possibility of seeking a career at sea, and that I should have to go home first to make my point at least, and indeed to see what other possibilities might exist. I also realized that in any case my absence would be reported to my parents and that I would have to face the consequences.

I tried to get a train to Worcester but was informed that the last through train of the day had left and there was only one going as far as Oxford. So I caught that one arriving at about 10 p.m. at

Oxford. This would allow me to catch the first train to Worcester the next day, which I did. However I was then faced with nowhere to sleep at Oxford since whatever money I had left after paying my ticket back to Worcester, I had to reserve to cover the rest of my fare from Worcester to Bredon station, in the village where I lived, and some refreshment on the way.

Thus I enquired from a friendly porter on Oxford station if there was somewhere where I could wait until the first train in the morning, and he said that as the waiting rooms would be closed I could use the staff room in the circumstances. This was to prove of lasting interest to me as the overnight staff were employed in parcel sorting from the numerous overnight mail trains, and I readily volunteered to give them a hand rather than sitting around doing nothing. In those days there were more lines into Oxford than nowadays, from Fairford for example, so there was a lot of this sort of traffic and it was a busy and fascinating night. Next day I continued my journey to Bredon, and arrived home to find that I had been reported as a missing under-age person and that the press had been informed.

It was obvious to me that the first thing I had to face on my return home was the disbelief of my parents that I could even consider doing such a thing, though their anger was tempered by the fact that I had returned on my own free will, and that I had come to no harm. (As a result of what was said to me at the time, I fully accepted that I should never have taken such action to make known my point. And indeed to this day I record for the sake of other families that young people should never follow my example and run away from school (or home), as there are other ways of protesting about one's treatment without causing distress to others, or for that matter endangering a young person's very existence). My father gave me a good talking to but strangely no chastisement, as I think that he was sensibly aware that my co-operation would be required if I was to stand a chance of getting back to Eton. Having failed in my mission to get to sea, I made it clear to him that I had nothing against Eton, in fact I had enjoyed my first Half (Term) there and had made some good friends, so that I would welcome being taken back by them. Perhaps I should mention that in those days, and I would imagine that the same thing applies nowadays, if a pupil ran away from school it would be unlikely that the school authorities would re-admit them, due to the obvious publicity such a case involves. The press in my case had given Eton the usual publicity that such an establishment always attracts, and which the school authorities naturally find vexing, so I did not rate my chances of getting back to be very good.

However my escapade was not based on funking life at boarding school, which is usually the case, and due to homesickness, but was based on seeking adventure. This was to be an important point in the persuasion of the school authorities to allow me back and was to form the basis of opinion expressed to the school authorities by an Old Etonian friend of my father's who lived near us at Elmley Castle just round Bredon Hill. I was then interviewed at short notice by the Late General Sir Francis Davies, a former Chief of the Imperial General Staff, and therefore an Old Etonian of undoubted influence. He naturally pointed out that I should not have taken the action that I had done to try and achieve a Naval career, but he admired my intention for the future to at least volunteer for service in the armed forces. He asked me very clearly whether I was prepared go back to Eton and serve the rest of my time there, upon which I was asked to give my solemn undertaking, and we shook hands upon it. I am glad to say that the General's intervention worked, and I was whisked back to Eton before the end of the week, and enjoyed the rest of my days there having what turned out to be an exceptional education. The General was a great local character, and I loved him always for what he did to give me the confidence to re-establish my life at Eton. (After the Second World War his son who took over the Elmley Castle estate on his father's death became a good friend of ours.)

The reception I got when I returned to school was mixed, as some of the friends I had made during the summer there thought that I had let the school down due to the publicity in the press. I had to accept this as something that I had not anticipated. But there were others who admired my pluck in having a go at proving what my ambition was. My Housemaster Mr C.E. Sladden was a very understanding man but made it clear to me that any other incident such as this and I would be out for good. I gave him my word that

I would settle down and finish my school education at Eton. I was advised that in fact there was a late entry scheme for the Royal Navy after public school education was finished so my ambition was still capable of achievement. So I set about enjoying what Eton had to offer, which was a great deal, as the school system was rather akin to a form of minor university in allowing a lot of freedom of choice in what one did.

The next and what later on turned out to be the greatest milestone in my life came very soon after I returned from Eton before Christmas that year. When I got home I found that I had been invited to a dance at the Swan Hotel Tewkesbury by two friends who had played tennis with me at Bredon, Pamela and Margaret Tetley, who lived at Redmarley, on the other side of Tewkesbury from us. The Swan Hotel was an old coaching inn and with a fine old ballroom, but sadly it is no more as the site has been redeveloped. Anyway I was there introduced to a girl that I had heard a lot of good things about, called Marylena Dyson Perrins, because she was at school with at least nine other girls that I knew in the Tewkesbury area, at Wychcrest School near the Wych cutting in Malvern. She was only a month younger than me, at the age of fourteen, and was very pretty and vivacious.

Indeed having had one dance with her I was so overcome with her charms that I tried to book her for most of the rest of the night (in those days we had dance programmes with the type of dance and number set out as it was ballroom dancing). For many years I kept that dance programme as evidence of the way that I had fallen for her, but I accidentally lost it sometime after the war. (It appears from a letter which my son Mark read out at our golden wedding in June 2000, written to him by one of Marylena's school friends at Wychcrest, Margaret Sandys (Davies), that in the following year, when I was 15, coming back from another dance in the car with her and Hugo Huntingdon-Whiteley (now Sir Hugo) I had stated that Marylena was the girl that I intended to marry. Whilst the intention may seem to have been very premature, strangely to say it seems that if the first love endures it is likely to be the best and remains so.) During the course of that first dance with Marylena at the Swan Hotel I told her that I had just gone back to Eton after running away to sea, and she listened to my story, and then exclaimed 'Well done, you have got spirit!' I knew then that at least I had made a new friend. Not all my other girl friends at the time thought likewise. I nevertheless put my foot in it literally as when going downstairs with her near the end of the night I trod on her very beautiful ballgown and tore the back of it, a matter that she has never let me forget as an example of my clumsiness.

In the summer of 1937 my family went with two of my female cousins and their parents on a motoring tour, starting in Sweden, then Denmark, and ending up in Germany, coming back from Bremerhaven on the SS *Bremen* to Southampton. Whilst staying at Travamunda on the Baltic it became quite clear from the manoevres going on with tanks and aircraft that Hitler was intent, having already annexed certain territories, on going to war, and so we of my generation at least would be involved before long.

So it was that my life over the next four years continued in the style to which I was accustomed, both at home and at College and University. I saw and frequently danced with Marylena on many occasions at parties around Worcestershire, up and until I joined the Royal Navy as a volunteer in March 1942. My admiration for Marylena remained paramount, in spite of there being many other attractive girls about in my part of the County. My problem of course was that she had a mass of other admirers consisting of many eligible young men, some of whom I knew well at school.

CHAPTER 2

College and university years

IT WAS NOT UNTIL I WENT TO CAMBRIDGE that I fully realized what an excellent and privileged education I had had. After getting over the initial minority response to my escapade, I settled down to what turned out to be a most enjoyable and on the whole unexceptional life at Eton College. I have stated 'on the whole' because, as I have already recorded, my mother being an artist and having taught me from an early age, and therefore having got Jack Nelson, my Prep School Headmaster, to give me extra tuition there, she repeated the order for the Eton School of Art. This came to nothing as the Eton Art department was going through what they now admit was a bad period under the Head of Art Mr Mengies Jones, who seemed to have more of an interest in puppets than anything else. In fact his puppet theatre has only just been recently demolished. A friend of mine there, the Late Tony Sandford, who later became an architect, and I managed to overcome this defect in the education to some extent because we both shared the same classical Tutor Mr N.G. Wykes and he offered to give us some extra art studies, which I will refer to in a later chapter.

Apart from this I found good company at Eton, some of which was to join me when I left and went on to Cambridge. There was much to occupy one's time there, including many unusual sports and games. The Wall Game, which to say the least was, and is, unique, I never partook in, except as a spectator. It was devised long before any other sport as far as I know, and consisted of a scrum against the College wall between a certain number of Scholars and the rest of us, termed the Oppidans. Except for continuing tradition it seemed pretty pointless to me. On the other hand the Field Game, also a unique Eton game, was a good one which I enjoyed playing. It was a mixture of soccer and rugby football, and much more interesting than either of those two games, which we occasionally played.

I liked cricket, but in my second Summer Term (known as a 'Half' at Eton) I transferred to being an oarsman (at Eton known as a 'Wet Bob'; a cricketer being known as a 'Dry Bob'), as due to the size of the school cricket was far more competitive than rowing, which I rightly assumed would be a rewarding and new experience. Even so as an oarsman it was not all that easy to become noticed in view of the numbers concerned. I loved sculling in my own rigger but never quite made it in my four seasons, though I made it through to the House Fours, and rowed for my House as number 2 (stroke side). During that period we did well in the races on the Thames. As to other activities there were plenty to occupy one's time, that is when one's studies allowed.

On the academic side the education could not be better, we were automatically put through a classical-based education, because in any case in those days you could not qualify for entry to Oxford or Cambridge Universities without a pass at least in Latin, even if you were to read such things as engineering, science, or medicine. As we had when entering Eton under the Common Entrance Exam to have at least a pass in Latin, and unusually in Latin Verse, this did not create problems. As the Romans were the founders of modern civilization, I must say that, however inconvenient it might be for modern academics to understand Latin, and Latin Verse for that matter, as this is an important side of artistic sense, the dropping of Latin as the foundation of university life and understanding does no good for civilization. Fortunately my preparatory school Arden House had given me an excellent grounding in the classical subjects as well as mathematics, which had enabled me to skip two forms when I entered Eton.

My Housemaster Mr C.E. Sladden happened to be the head Science Master, and as I was reasonably good at mathematics he took an interest in pushing me along in the sciences, particularly in physics and chemistry, and this we shall see was to play a significant part in my life in the Royal Navy. Indeed when faced with the exams to qualify for a university education he made me study under a chemistry tutor friend of his, Mr S. Bastin, in the holidays at the Cheltenham Technical College. Otherwise he said that I would probably not pass in chemistry. In the event when I took the exams I got credits rather than passes in all subjects, and in practical chemistry was the only pupil nationally on that occasion to obtain 100% marks. Cyril Sladden was absolutely delighted, and it was a great tribute to his efforts as well as the Eton system of education.

When I came to leave Eton I found that a place had been offered to me by Magdalen College Oxford, however as I had passed the entrance exams at a high level I was also offered a place at Trinity College Cambridge. I took the latter as my elder brother John was at Magdalene College Cambridge, and furthermore a number of my Friends at Eton were going on to Cambridge, at least three of them to Trinity.

So I took up residence in digs near Trinity College for the start of the Spring Term 1941, having already been interviewed by my Tutor Professor Patrick ('Plum') Duff, whom I liked from the very start, a good beginning! My brother John had returned to Magdalene college with me, and so was able to show me around the city and help me settle in, which was a great advantage. However as I have already related a number of my friends from Eton went up at the same time, so immediately we started our own table in Hall and dined together. It was also fortunate for me that an old Harrovian friend of my brother and I lived in our village at Bredon, and was already in his third year at Trinity College, and so he introduced me to quite a number of old Harrovians there, some of whom became firm friends for life. We had a table of splendid undergraduates, half of whom sadly did not survive the subsequent inevitable service during World War II. Most notable was a dear friend and old Harrovian Leslie Widdowson who served in the Scots Guards at Monte Cassino, and like so many others never returned. He and I thought much the same about things, and enjoyed shooting together and playing tennis and the humour of life. Sadly my thoughts always move to him, amongst others, on every Armistice Day. But there it is, those of my table who survived realized that we had to be thankful for that, and that we had had a damned good time at Cambridge, a wonderful place. The College shoot out near Duxford was some of the best that I have had in the last 65 years. The rowing was fun and I found myself rowing at no 2 in the First and Third Trinity 1st eight as soon as I joined. The Third Trinity Boat Club, which specialized in coxless pairs, closed down because of the lack of support whilst I was there, so that I must have been one of the last members. I have still got their very smart tie and blazer.

There was a good social life as well at Cambridge with plenty of dinner parties, dances and bump suppers. Indeed it was in my final term in November 1941, that an Harrovian friend of mine, Graham Allen, held a roulette party in our adjoining rooms in the ground floor of K staircase in Great Court (now a Don's residence) and it got slightly out of hand! Apparently some of our guests from other Colleges had decided spice the party up a bit before they left, and proceeded to do a dance around the Fountain in great Court, which resulted in all the plants around the fountain being damaged. Graham and I were hauled up before the Dean, Mr Rattenbury, and rightly ordered to replace the plants. We had been totally unaware of this very unfriendly act of our guests, as some of us were still playing roulette, and we made this clear to the Dean. We therefore deemed it very unfair that the Dean ordered that we should be sent down for one term as a punishment. This sentence meant, at that particular time, as the War was on, that we would automatically be called up, and that our respective studies would be interrupted, probably never to be resumed. Whilst we were obtaining a degree we had been classified as in a reserved occupation. My Tutor Professor Duff told me, when I met him soon after the War, that he thought at the time that this was a great injustice to Graham and myself, and had said so then. He was so glad to see that we had both by God's mercy survived, and said that he would ensure that Trinity College would always invite us back when appropriate, which they have done to this day. I attended a May Ball after the War and have attended a number of reunion dinners also.

However life is full of set backs, and both Graham and I had already signed on for the Volunteer Reserves, he the Army, and myself for the Navy, as we knew by that time that it was likely to go on for a long time, thus we were not worried about this decision except for the effect it would have on our parents and our subsequent careers if we survived the War. One amusing part of the whole event was that as Graham's rooms were to be used for the roulette, mine were used as the bar. We had invited a very large number of our undergraduate friends in the University in general. So we asked a friend whose family ran a local brewery to supply a 36-gallon barrel of beer together with a bar, beer engine, and spirit dispensers, which he did. We wanted to do the thing properly, the only trouble being that instead of concentrating on the roulette some of the guests spent too much time in our professionally run bar. After having dealt with us for having a disorderly party on College premises, the Dean said he had always wanted to have a beer engine in his rooms when giving a party, could we tell him where we managed to get one of those from!

CHAPTER 3

The start of war service in the Royal Navy

I VOLUNTEERED FOR THE RNVR at the Cambridge recruiting office before leaving Cambridge under the RNY entry scheme which offered fast track promotion to University educated people. I therefore arrived home in November 1941 from Cambridge as a Naval recruit waiting to be ordered to join HMS *Ganges* which was the nearest training base to Cambridge.

My father was far from pleased, to say the least, at my return, having been sent down, a matter of which he was already aware of course. However he said that he had anticipated that I would be called up because of the war, as he had been in 1914, so he had arranged with my cousin Captain Ian Liddell (later a VC) of the Coldstream Guards, as I had been in the OTC at Eton and obtained my Cert. A. qualification, for me to be granted a Commission in his Regiment. I thanked him but stated that I had already joined the Royal Navy. He was very upset that I had done this, as he had never forgiven the Navy for having appeared to let the Army down in evacuating the men from Gallipoli where his brother had perished on the beaches. However there was nothing he could do about it thankfully as I was signed on. So having Christmas at home there was time for adjustment. As the Admiralty had ordered me to serve in the Home Guard pending having a place at HMS *Ganges*, I was kept occupied in the war effort until early in March, when I received an order to join that training establishment, which is famous in the Royal Navy because you have to learn to climb a 143ft mast and dress it before you leave to go to sea.

At the end of February 1942 I had received my railway warrant and order to report at a certain time on the Quay at Harwich harbour, where I was met along with the others joining that week by a very civil and polite Chief Petty Officer, and asked get into a

Mast at Shotley is to be refurbished

ONE of Suffolk's best-known landmarks is to be missing for part of the summer.

The task of dismantling the huge mast at the former HMS Ganges Naval training base at Shotley is due to be completed today. The work began on Saturday.

The 143-foot mast is to be completely refurbished by the new owners of the site, Potton Development Ltd, and should be back on site at the end of June.

It has dominated Shotley for more than 80 years and until Ganges closed in 1976 was used for displays by Naval cadets.

Since then little has been done to maintain it, but now it is to be completely restored.

The base is metal, but the rest of the mast is wood and the rope rigging also needs to be replaced.

Much of the work is expected to take place on site and it is expected to cost between £30,000 and £40,000 to complete.

"The mast is the best-known landmark around here and Potton's see it as the centrepiece for the village they plan to build on this site," said Eurosports Village manager Mr. Terry Houlden.

"It was very well maintained by the Navy, but this will be the first time that the mast has been completely refurbished since it was erected."

The HMS Ganges Association contributed more than £6,000 towards the refurbishment work and when it is returned plan to dedicate it to former trainees.

"We hope to unveil a plaque dedicating it to everyone who passed through Ganges and lost his life in Naval service," said Mr. Dicky Doyle of the association.

"There will be a full dedication service with a band and parade, it will be very good to see it back to its full glory."

Riggers dismantling the mast at the former HMS Ganges training base at Shotley on Saturday.

Extract from East Anglian Times *18 April 1988*

steam driven harbour launch. We arrived on the other side of the estuary at Shotley pier whereupon the Chief Petty Officer completely changed his style, and announced that we were in the Navy now, and bellowed at us to fall in line abreast. Thus the well known standard of Naval discipline started for me. We marched up to the annex to the main Barracks where we were to spend a week being issued with uniforms and having medical checks, including the one which has been the subject of comedians' jokes for many decades, as well need I say as being marched endlessly up and down by the Petty Officers. The food during that first week was the worst that I came across in the Royal Navy, where the general standard of food on the whole was good or acceptable, and well monitored by the Officers. I was therefore glad when that first week was over, and we were marched over into the main Barracks of *Ganges* and handed over to the Petty Officers in charge of our Mess were we would be for the next 12 weeks.

Much has been written about the harshness of the training at HMS *Ganges*, but what are we to expect in such an establishment. In my own experience at school one was used to discipline and to me it was no more than expected. The Chief Petty Officer in charge of my mess was a good instructor, and indeed his Assistant Petty Officer was a splendid instructor, particularly in teaching us all the knots and splices, I have never forgotten what he taught us. I would say that the loss of privacy, which service life involves and we accept, and the climbing before breakfast of the famous 143ft mast were the only disadvantages in being at Shotley Barracks.

The mast, which is still preserved to the present day, seemed awe-inspiring to most of us until we got used to it. We were allowed for the first few weeks to climb the first set of shrouds only, if we wished, and to go through the 'Lubbers Hole', but thereafter we were required to climb outside the rigging onto the second set of shrouds. This involved going up or down on the return at a backwards angle of 45 degrees to the ground, a matter which to even a young man like me was a cause of a great deal of fear, even though we had practised climbing at such an angle in the gym previously. (I remember on a visit to Shotley Point about 15 years ago, where there is now a marina, the Manager saying to me, on hearing that I had trained there many years ago, 'I do not know how you chaps managed to climb over that mast!' My reply was that the Admiralty had devised excellent methods of persuasion in the form of Petty Officers, and furthermore the training before breakfast ensured that Admiralty resources were not needlessly wasted due to fright!). One has to remember that this mast is similar to those which were in use at sea in the days of sail, though I believe we were one of the few training establishments with one left. So it was very good training for men to have to go aloft, and I shall be referring to this later on in this story.

So there we are, 12 weeks of intensive training at *Ganges* with a run ashore by bus into Ipswich each week. Life was interesting and enjoyable. We had when on Duty Watch to man the trenches and other defences outside the Barracks. For this purpose we were issued with pikes consisting of a bayonet stuck in the end of a metal pole. This we were informed was because there was a general shortage of service rifles due to the losses at Dunkirk, and the stores were waiting for replacements; however our section leaders were allowed to draw a rifle, so I pretty soon made it my business to become a section leader! In the Home Guard, which I had only just left behind, we all had American 300 service rifles and ammunition instead of British service rifles, so the situation in the Senior Service was difficult to follow. The only events that disturbed our routine were the air attacks which happened fairly regularly (but as the whole Harwich area was a Naval Base with Destroyers and Corvettes nearby it was well defended), and the incident of the Hunt Class Destroyer HMS *Cotswold*, which had to beach on the point at Shotley, aptly known as Bloody Point, after hitting a mine. This had blown a hole in a boiler room with consequent casualties. I was on Duty Watch when this happened and we had to bring the casualties up the beach into the very good Hospital at *Ganges*. I was then ordered to hold the hand of one of the Stokers from the *Cotswold* and talk to him on his way out. He had been steam scalded on the chest and his lungs had been laid bare. It was a dreadful duty, but one that would condition me for what was to come.

We were sent on leave for a week after the passing out parade, and I was then ordered to report to HMS *Pembroke*, namely Chatham Barracks. I returned home feeling very proud of my new

Naval uniform of an Ordinary Seaman, though my father had not yet come to terms with my non-commissioned state. In fact whilst I was at *Ganges*, he had contacted the First Sea Lord Admiral Sir Dudley Pound, who was a friend of the family, and said, ' My son David has joined the Navy – kindly see that he is looked after.' I was then hauled in front of the *Ganges* Captain RN of Barracks, as a signal had been sent to him, and asked for an explanation. I told him that I was unaware of this approach of which I would not have approved. The Captain dismissed me though he told me not to expect any privilege being granted to me in the Royal Navy, in spite of whom I happened to know. He also added that they did not particularly like old Etonians in the service for this reason, which I considered very unfair. I felt that my Admiralty record must have been adversely endorsed at an early stage for this reason, and as a result felt that my father was accountable. Though I have to say that later on in the Service I had an evident endorsement which may have proved much more to my detriment, and which caused me merriment many years later, and which I will relate in due course.

It seems to me that a shortage of trained men in early 1942 was apparent due to casualties and the accelerated Naval building programme necessary after two years of war. Anyway after my 12 weeks of excellent training, I was only stationed in Chatham Barracks for a few weeks before being drafted to HMS *Kent*, a County Class heavy eight-inch gun Cruiser. This was a relief because those barracks were overcrowded due to wartime conditions, and the use of the tunnels for sleeping in was not very pleasant.

Except for a long weekend leave, we were occupied in doing various odd jobs around the place. One day I was detailed to tend the bonfire in the Commodore's garden. There were however three experiences which I found interesting. I was sent with a squad one day down to the famous Chatham Dockyard to clean the bottom of the dry dock in which the famous light Cruiser HMS *Ajax* was undergoing a refit. Fortunately, for it was an extremely hot June day, there was very little sweeping up work to be done, so we went for an early lunch in the canteen aboard *Ajax* where we were well received by the skeleton crew. We had a

Leading Seaman in charge of our small squad and as we had done most of the work before lunch, he allowed us, as by now it was extremely hot in the bottom of that dry dock, to have a rest on the unused keel blocks under HMS *Ajax*, having posted a lookout, just in case an Officer or worse still a Petty Officer turned up. So I had an interesting day seeing close up one of the ships that took part in the Battle of the River Plate.

Another matter of interest to me was a visit ordered as a study of what we in the Navy were up against. It so happened that a captured U-Boat 570 was in one of the dry docks being refitted for service in the Royal Navy, and had been renamed HMS *Graph*. We were shown over this and I must say it was very impressive. As these boats had to operate over long periods and distances, they were much larger than our own, and had better accommodation, no wonder they caused us more trouble at sea than anything else.

The only other event of note whilst I was at Chatham, other than the inevitable air raids, was the escorting of a number of deserters who had been found guilty by Court Martial. On one exceptionally hot June day, on falling in for morning divisions in the Drill Hall, some of us were selected to parade separately as a prisoner escort. The deserters were duly marched in after divisions had ceased. The Barrack Boatswain, who was a Commissioned Gunnery Officer (that is that he had two thick rings on his arm like a Lieutenant RN), fell us in either side of the column of deserters. He then addressed the parade, and told us that he was a real bastard and if any prisoner should try to escape before being handed over to the military authorities for punishment we were to bayonet them with the weapons just issued to us as their escorts. He declared that he had served in the First World War and then all deserters were shot if the Courts Martial found them guilty. However he went on to say that in this war their Lordships of the Admiralty had decided in their wisdom to discharge them from the the service after severe punishment in the 'glasshouse', a decision he did not necessarily agree with. The death penalty is a debatable subject in peacetime, but as I was due under orders to inflict it on the Germans subsequently in wartime, what the Officer said one felt in agreement with. Anyhow I can relate that any move to escape would without any doubt have involved us in the immediate use of our arms. We fellows in the Navy detested any form of cowardice or desertion.

We were then ordered to embark on a large Naval troop-carrying lorry, where we sat each side of our respective prisoners, and I can tell you that my hand never left my bayonet, as the Boatswain had told us before the prisoners joined us that it was a regulation that if the prisoners were allowed to escape, we personally would have to serve their sentences until they were recaptured. I had no intention of putting myself in that situation, as I was about to have some leave before joining the ship that I had been drafted to already.

We were driven up to the Army run 'Glasshouse' near Gillingham in the by now sweltering heat, where we handed over our cowards to the Military Police and a very fierce Sergeant Major. We could see the inmates being doubled up and down in the extreme heat, and knew that when our prisoners had done their time there they had been treated to a deserved punishment. Having handed over, the Regulating Petty Officer in charge of us told to stand easy whilst waiting for the lorry to take us back, and we were standing chatting when a very irate Colonel emerged and had us called to attention. He then gave us a dressing down for being sloppy and stated that he would report this to the Naval Authorities at Chatham. I am glad to say however that nothing further was done about it, and so I assume it was the Army making clear their superiority over us, as was then the fashion before combined forces had appeared.

Soon after that occasion I was issued with a Railway warrant by the drafting office at HMS *Pembroke*, and ordered to join my first ship HMS *Kent* in Cammell Laird's dry dock at Birkenhead. I was glad to be leaving Chatham for the time being.

CHAPTER 4

HMS *Kent* and the refit before joining the Russian convoys

A T THE BEGINNING OF JULY 1942 I joined the County Class Heavy Cruiser HMS *Kent* at Birkenhead, where she was having a long refit due to having been damaged in action, and also being fitted with the very latest Radar ready for service on the Russian Convoys.

So there I was, Ordinary Seaman Cottrell, a CW (Commission Warrant, as I was recruited under the Y scheme to give fast promotion) rating standing with my kit on the side of No 2 dry dock at Cammell Laird's yard about to board ship. In spite of the usual dockyard litter when a ship is under refit, I thought that this great 10,000-ton ship looked magnificent, and I was not only glad but proud to join her. I reported to the duty Quartermaster as directed by the Marine Sentry and was told to go to the regulating office amidships to sign on. I had been allocated to the Port Watch of the Maintop Division, and was shown the way to their Mess (living quarters) on the portside forward abreast of A Turret (being the forward turret). This was to be my home for the next eleven months.

Even though I was a Chatham Rating, and a CW one at that, I received a good welcome in the Mess which was fully in operation as only the Starboard Watch was on leave at the time. I was to learn that even though the ship was the largest ever built in Chatham Dockyard, she was a Devonport manned vessel. Indeed the crew were nearly all regulars of the Navy, most of whom had served in her when she was Flagship of the China Station. One of my messmates was asked by the Leading Seaman in charge of the mess to show me round the ship, which was spacious, and I chose to sling my hammock that night and thereafter above the engine room in the fore cabin flat.

Apparently the ship had been torpedoed in the bow by an Italian submarine off Bardia, which she was ordered to bombard on her way back from China, she had been beached and a temporary repair made to enable her to get to Gibraltar for more substantial repairs to get round to Devonport. Whilst in Devonport being refitted she had a stick of bombs put through the forecastle and further repairs were carried out. Next the ship was sent up to the Arctic, but with the heavy seas up there causing forecastle leaks, and her lack of steam heating, she was found to be unsuitable for the Arctic operations. The ship was returned therefore to Birkenhead for the forecastle deck and plating to be renewed, and steam heating to be fitted. At the same time Asdic (Sonar) and the very latest Radar were to be fitted. On hearing all this I could understand why so much work was going on, and why a refit, which had already taken three months, was necessary during a war.

The next day I fell in at morning divisions for the first time. Our Maintop Division was commanded by Lt Henley RN (later Vice Admiral), who was away on leave, and we had two Petty Officers. The one in charge PO Whitlock was also away, so Petty Officer Phippin was in charge, he was the nice one! The First Lieutenant, Lt Commander Peter Agnew RN Retrd MP, was the Executive Officer on board and took the parade on the main deck amidships on the starboard side. He was an exceptionally nice Officer, and the crew held him in very high regard. (I will relate later how after the war he came to live next door to us and we became great friends.) I was detailed off to go painting on the superstructure under the supervision of a Leading Seaman, which over much of the time until we sailed from Liverpool seemed to be the principal work in hand, except when it was raining when we painted below.

We got shore leave every other day so had plenty of time to explore Birkenhead and Liverpool and the surrounding area such as New Brighton, where there was an excellent dance hall full of girls wanting to dance with sailors. There was no doubt about the support of Liverpool people for the Navy, as we were to find out when we left there.

We had the Cruiser HMS *Cleopatra* which was an improved Dido Class cruiser being finished off as a new ship in the next dock. What a really lovely design for a warship! In addition Cammells had a new destroyer being launched every three weeks or thereabouts. Though our admiration of this effort was tempered by the behaviour of some of the dockyard workers who had apparently been slowing production for a generation by holding what were known as hole boring disputes between their various Unions. In the case of these new ships the management had found the answer, they had installed the most enormous hydraulic presses in the yard, which cut out the holes in the bulkheads in the course of production.

Even so these hypocritical workers, who were constantly holding hole boring disputes on our ship, thus preventing us from returning to the Fleet, would down tools on every launching to go and cheer the new ship down the slipway. As they were working on the fitting of the numerous cables required to be run about our ship for the new Radar installations, as well as the steam heating, we seemed to have our accommodation taken up during the daytime for their card playing, which we much resented. Since I gather such disputes had been going on for years, and, it seems, continued after the war, it is amazing that the yard managed to remain in business. In the previous year the Germans had dropped on Birkenhead a line of parachute mines with the intention of hitting the dockyard, and the wind blew them inshore on to the workers' houses on the other side of the road, yet the losses sustained failed to overcome the prolonging of the war effort by the two Unions involved.

Whilst in the dry dock one incident occurred that was indirectly, but thankfully, to affect my whole career in the Navy (the explanation of which I will come to in a later chapter). The First Lieutenant, Lt Commander Peter Agnew, was just after lunch down in the dry dock with the Dockyard Chief inspecting the repairs to the ship's bottom. The Commander was in his number one rig about to go on leave later that day. There was a very nice New Zealand Rating, who had only the week before joined the ship, in the Mess next door to ours. He was apparently unaware of the dry dock regulations. So it was that after lunch (Messdeck dinner) instead of taking the Mess bucket of gash (swill) ashore, he ditched it out of the porthole next to our Mess, and it so happened it landed on top of the Commander and Dockyard Chief standing directly below. The Commander, after the duty Officer had seen to his clean up, descended on to our Messdeck and demanded that the culprit be revealed or else the whole of the Port Watch of our Division would suffer the loss of leave for a week. Us chaps including the Leading Seamen held our peace and so suffered the consequences. Anyway as our pay was too little to sustain so much life ashore all the while, being only one shilling and sixpence per day for an Ordinary Seaman and two shillings and sixpence for an Able Seaman, most of us did not go ashore every day anyway when we were not on Duty Watch.

So for about the first month that I was on board we continued to work on the ship in the dry dock, until such time as the forecastle had been repaired and the torpedo hole in the bottom replated as well as the painting of the bottom. Then the Admiralty had us towed out of the dry dock across the River Mersey into the Gladstone Dock at Liverpool. For this movement our Captain, who was Captain Angus Cunninghame Graham RN (later Admiral Sir Angus Cunninghame Graham DSO), was on board, and we had our first Captain's inspection when he welcomed us new members of his crew. It was a relief being in Gladstone Dock because we had new contractors finishing off the ship without further hole boring disputes. So our Messdeck became ours again without strikers playing cards! With the overhead railway, alas now long since gone, we were able to go ashore into Liverpool very easily, though we had to catch a ferry or go by train to New Brighton, but this only took a little while longer.

As the ship neared completion we were sprouting new Radar cabins and aerials, therefore it came as less of a surprise when the CinC of Western Approaches, Admiral Sir Percy Noble, came aboard to inspect us just before we left Liverpool and addressed us about it. He stated that we were one of the most up-to-date Radar ships in the Royal Navy, and that we were designed give the Germans in the Arctic waters a 'Bloody Nose'. He wished us the best of luck in doing so and had no doubt that the Radar would ensure our success.

CHAPTER 5

HMS *Kent* in the Arctic and on Russian convoys

IN SEPTEMBER 1942 WE LEFT GLADSTONE DOCK, LIVERPOOL bound for the Home Fleet main base at Scapa Flow in the Orkney Islands north of Scotland. As the ship was towed out of the dock we were fallen in to dress ship, which meant that according to which Division one was in, there was where you stood. My Division being the Maintop Division was therefore amidships. The Marine Band was on the quarterdeck playing the customary tunes for such occasions, 'Land of Hope and Glory' and 'Rule Britannia' etc. The dockside was lined with an amazingly large crowd cheering us on the way, showing us what we meant to Liverpool. I have to admit that as I feared that it might have been my last sight of England in view of the daunting task ahead of us in the Arctic War, I felt the occasion was a proud moment never to be forgotten.

I was allocated a sea station to start with on the air defence platform abaft the Conning platform on the Bridge, as my gunnery knowledge acquired at *Ganges* had not been assessed. I had known the turbulence of the Irish Sea from the days on board my grandfather's 820-ton yacht as he proceeded round Scotland. Needless to say the sea, as we proceeded out of the Mersey, was boisterous, with one of the well known gales north of there blowing, good for getting one's sea-legs again. Being on duty as a lookout I got a good view of the Isle of Man as we passed it, and I have not had occasion to see it since. So the ship duly joined the Home Fleet then commanded by Admiral Tovey at Scapa Flow.

For several weeks thereafter we were engaged in working up exercises with the other units of the fleet, which were then on standby as reserve units. I well remember the first Sunday divisions (Church Parade) on board. The *Kent* was fitted as a flagship, and we were designated the Flagship of the First Cruiser Squadron, having just relieved HMS *Cumberland* if I remember rightly, so

Admiral Hamilton and his staff had joined us and we were all the more formal. Thus as the weather was good the ship's company of just over 700 strong were fallen in on the quarterdeck complete with the marine band. We were given the usual Admiralty hymn card whilst standing at ease, and the Chaplin gave out the number of the opening hymn. This was Admiralty hymn number 1, 'Eternal Father Strong to Save', which as a lad I had been taught by heart. On parade we were still expected to dress our hymn cards at an angle of 45 degrees, quite rightly as we prided ourselves in the Navy in always being smart and well disciplined. Unfortunately due to my familiarity with the words of that famous hymn, my card dipped right down without me thinking about it. Petty Officer Whitlock had my name taken, and I was run in before the Officer of the Watch after the service and given seven days work in the galley during the dogwatches peeling spuds as a punishment.

When I returned to the Messdeck before lunch I described my fate, much to my messmates' merriment, but there was a Scot there who was previously aware of the fact that I was of half Scottish ancestry, and in consequence addressed me as 'Jock', who said I should join the Church of Scotland and so avoid such parades in future. He being a regular Able Seaman Rating and therefore knowing all the ropes told me to put in a request to the Divisional Officer to change my religion as we were berthed within Scottish Waters and therefore the Church facilities were on hand ashore. I duly appeared before Lieutenant Henley RN , whom I always felt was a very nice Officer and very understanding. I explained that my mother's parents were of Scottish descent (here he asked for their name), and as I was in Scottish waters I was keen to join their Church. He stated that my request seemed reasonable in the circumstances, and to my astonishment granted it. However he made it clear that regulations only allowed for one change in religion, and so that for the rest of my time in the Service I would be an official member of the Church of Scotland. Needless to say I was highly delighted because thereafter I was ordered to fall out and get into the drifter along with the Roman Catholics and other dissenting Church parties to go ashore to worship in peace.

I have to relate the other benefits beyond just the freedom from falling in for Church Parades, which unless I desired to do so lasted my time in the service, and these whilst in the Fleet at Scapa Flow were of great advantage. As my Able Seaman friend had described to me when we disembarked from the drifter, which was a steamship used as a ferry and storeship, we had a short service in the Church of Scotland hut on Flotta Island, followed by buns and coffee dished out by the church helpers. By that time the fleet canteen on Flotta had opened and we had an hour in the bar and time for several drinks before catching the drifter back to the ship. On returning to our Messdeck we found our lunch served up for us, and our mates had drawn our daily tot of grog (rum). I was therefore lucky to have had a Scottish connection and also a good Scottish pal on the Messdeck!

The first few weeks at Scapa Flow were taken up with gunnery practice at sea and manoeuvres with the reserve ships of the Battle Fleet. What was most interesting was that when the ordinary form of gunnery by director was used it could not get anywhere close to the accuracy of the firing by Radar, so the new Radar sets fitted in Liverpool filled us with confidence. It was interesting to me to be on a ship which was one of the first to use for gunnery purposes, this then amazing British invention which played such a key defence role in the Services during that war. This interest was, as we shall see later, to be of significance for me when I was transferred to the technical side of the Radar Division of the Royal Navy and ended up as a Radar instructor at HMS *Collingwood* at Fareham.

Being a CW Rating during this working up period, I was ordered to serve in several different positions in the ship including the magazine and shell handling room of the eight-inch guns, and also as a loading number on the four-inch guns amidships. The latter position was somewhat testing, as being fixed ammunition, when the gun fired and the shell case was ejected, not only did one get a flash out of the breach, but if you were not quick in catching the shell case the chances were that you had a sore foot! Those four-inch guns seemed always to make the most noise as well. However I managed to pass muster on these various training positions and graduated to the dome teacher and anti aircraft gunnery, thereby being introduced to the Oerliken Gun which was easy to use and I think the best of the anti-aircraft guns.

During our manoeuvres with the Fleet off the Shetland and Orkneys we found ourselves steaming parallel to the 35,000-ton Battleship *King George V*, Admiral Tovey's Flagship, in a heavy sea. I was on duty as a look out on the starboard side of the Air Defence Position on the Bridge when suddenly HMS *Matchless*, a new Fleet Destroyer of 1900 tons, built in 1940 and with crew of 200, which was the escort to the *King George V* appeared steaming at full speed ahead of us to starboard turned across our bows. Our Captain rang down 'Stop engines', which as we were doing our full speed of 32 knots (36 mph) only reduced our speed by a fraction, the Destroyer was of course faster by several knots but we only just missed her. I must say I held my breath as the Destroyer's stern disappeared under our bows. It was a near miss, like many others during the war, the heavy sea running no doubt contributing to the problems on the Destroyer. I recall that the 35,000-ton *King George V* was rolling her bilge keels out of the water at the time, however I do not doubt that a court of enquiry was held aboard her when we returned to Scapa Flow, as the result of a collision had it happened would have been a major disaster.

During this working up period volunteers were called for among the lookouts to man the crow's nest, because when going in and out of the fleet anchorage we had to stream paravanes, which are heavy torpedo-shaped floats strung off chains on the cutting edge of the ship's bow, to cut adrift any mines and therefore to reduce speed, thus we were much more liable to U-Boat attack. The best place to spot a periscope was in the crow's nest. As a Devonport manned ship there were not many chaps trained to climb aloft, particularly in rough weather, so the few of us Chatham men trained on the mast at *Ganges* came into our own, and could show off our skills to the others on board, so that volunteers were forthcoming. I found it exciting in the crow's nest, particularly in the Pentland Firth between Scapa and the mainland, as you got an amazing view all around up there and you felt that you owned the ship. As one climbed the Jacob's Ladder up into the crow's nest as the ship rolled you swung out over the sea, and so it was a good thing that they taught us the correct armlock, which is the one trapeze artists use, at HMS *Ganges*.

With reference to the Pentland Firth, where there is frequently a tide race running, on one occasion when we were moored inside

HMS King George V

Scapa Flow and HMS *Bermuda*, another Cruiser, was streaming paravanes, the ship's chief Executive Officer, a Commander RN and about 30 men were washed overboard in the rough seas and under the propellors. A terrible tragedy, but as nearly always, it was due to the sea conditions, a necessary and hazardous task for all ships. The problem being that a ship had to be doing at least 14 knots to enable the paravanes to operate, and so in rough conditions it was easy to ship a lot of water over the forecastle.

During this working up period we did a lot of gunnery instruction and practice. This included firing our main eight-inch guns at sleeve targets towed by an aircraft. We could elevate these guns up to an angle of 70 degrees, and the ship had been fitted in Liverpool with a Radar set that could control the main armament. So this new development was tried out, by first firing under the old director-controlled gunnery, and then firing by Radar. As was to be expected the Radar got the target every time the guns were fired, whereas the traditional form of gunnery calculation could not compete. Thus what Admiral Sir Percy Noble had said to us in Liverpool gave us some confidence that on meeting the German airforce off Norway we might indeed give them a hard time.

On one occasion when coming to our buoy in the fleet anchorage in a gale I was detailed by Petty Officer Whitlock to fall in for the buoy jumping party as it was the Maintop Division's turn to carry out this task. One of the frequent gales in that sea area was blowing, so when the three of us jumped onto the buoy, the seas were breaking over the top of it. There were three of us involved: a Blacksmith to deal with the shackle, a Leading Seaman in charge, and myself, an Ordinary Seaman. We were taken up to the buoy in the motor cutter, which stood by to take us off as soon as the ship was connected to the buoy.

The buoy was a large one but on the tilt due to the wind and rough sea. As the ship moved up to it very slowly indeed we had to hold the anchor cable whilst the Blacksmith put the pin of the shackle through the ring of the buoy, thus securing the ship. It was a tricky job at the best of times for the Captain and forecastle Officers to get the bow into the correct position. On this occasion because of the gale when the ship came up to us the first time the First Lieutenant and Chief Boatswain's Mate admonished us because we had to let the cable go, since it was too tight for the Blacksmith to put the pin through the ring, and with 10,000 tons of ship on the other end there was no way in which we could hold on.

The next time the ship approached we had the Chief Officer Commander Oswald in addition shouting at us and we missed again, whereupon the shouting, which it was difficult to hear because of the gale, increased, and to my horror our Leading Seaman swore back at them. I said to him stop it or we will be run aft and charged when we get on board. He replied that I need not worry because anything we shouted would be lost under the bows in the wind, so we swore back at them, what an opportunity! The ship had to come up twice more before we got the pin in. Then the Chief Botswain's Mate told us with a loud hailer that the launch had been withdrawn because of our failure of duty, and that we would have to climb up the anchor cable through the hawse pipe on to the forecastle. Since the forecastle was about 30ft above the waterline, and the cable of course was at about a 30 degree angle, this was quite a climb, at times I wondered if I could make it.

The three of us arrived back on the forecastle to be met by the Boatswain's Mate, who tore a strip off us for incompetence and ran us in down aft before the Officer of the Watch in the Quartermaster's lobby. We were charged with dereliction of duty and, because we were covered in rust as well as being soaking wet, being improperly dressed. I am glad to say that the Officer, who of course was on the bridge at the time, said that he took into account the weather conditions, and the fact that we had been made to climb up the anchor cable which was punishment enough, and dismissed the charges. Like most Naval Officers he was a decent man. I heard afterwards that the CinC had signalled from HMS *King George V* 'are you having difficulties?' and this had in turn caused the unusual attention to our activities under the bow. Such a signal from the flagship always caused consternation. I remember being told by a Destroyer Captain after the war that his crew misread a signal when the flotilla turned at speed and he turned the ship the opposite way to the rest. The Commander of the flotilla signalled 'what the hell are you doing?' and he signalled back 'am learning very fast'.

However such a reply to Admiral Tovey in particular might not be greeted with a laugh. Later on when Admiral Fraser took command of the fleet it could well have been, because as I will relate he was a humorist, as well as a fine leader.

One day in Scapa Flow the duty watch spotted a young female seal alongside the ship trying to get on board as she was affected by fuel oil. They lifted her on board for the medics to clean her up, which took several days, and in the meantime the crew made a fuss of her. When she was fit to be released she swam around and caught some fish, and to everyone's surprise asked to be taken aboard again. The Captain's permission was asked and given and so she took up residence in the forward lobby, being lowered over the side each day when the ship was in harbour to go and fish. When we were at sea we had to feed her on frozen fish stores. She became the ship's mascot and received a lot of fuss from us who used to stroke her and talk to her. Eventually after several months we docked in Glasgow for minor repairs and the Captain arranged to hand her over to the Glasgow Zoo, who were delighted. Since we were at sea a lot I think that she needed rather a lot of fish stores and so this opportunity for her long-term wellbeing was sensibly taken. But we all missed her as by that time she had become a pet, and was most intelligent.

The only other event of interest during this time was the delivery on board of a huge wire net which remained for a while on the main deck near the crane amidships. Apparently it was an anti-human torpedo net for protection whilst at anchor. So one day the whole seaman's division was mustered amidships and ordered to exercise against a human torpedo attack. So all of us had to spread this net out along the whole ship's length and then dump it over the side. For some reason those in charge had forgotten that the ship had four propellers and the outside ones protruded beyond the ship's side down aft. In consequence we had dumped part of the net over the outer starboard propellor and so it was jammed on the propeller and would not budge when we proceeded to try and recover the net. Thus the ship was out of action for at least two days whilst the Divers cut the net away. The CinC was not pleased and came aboard to inspect the situation. Thankfully the remains of the net were taken away after that and not replaced.

At last the working up of the ship was complete, Rear Admiral Hamilton and his staff came aboard and we became Flagship of the First Cruiser Squadron, and a frontline ship of the Home Fleet.

HMS *Berwick*, a sister ship, joined us and we steamed up to Iceland with a convoy, and which then went through to Murmansk. The first major action that involved us was at the end of December 1942 when on standby back in Scapa Flow we got an emergency Fleet order from the CinC to put to sea within twenty minutes at best speed to intercept and engage the German Pocket Battleship *Lutzow* and Cruiser *Hipper* off the coast of Norway as they had been engaged by HMS *Sheffield* and HMS *Jamaica* guarding a convoy, and were heading South. We steamed at full speed to Norway off the Lofoten Islands, where we hoisted our battle ensigns on obtaining a Radar contact from two ships. A radio challenge was sent out twice with no answer and the Gunnery Officer gave the order to standby to turn and fire a broadside to starboard. I felt, along with others, that we were about to suffer a glorious end as three Cruisers, one with eight-inch guns, had a job with dealing with the *Graf Spee*, a sister ship of the *Lutzow*, simply because their guns would outrange us. However a final challenge was answered; it was the *Sheffield* and *Jamaica* coming towards us. We were in a heavy sea and blizzard and understandably this was affecting radio communications with the Admiralty and other ships. So our moment of excitement was over as the Germans had evidently retreated into their base at Trondheim. We hauled down our huge battle white ensigns and returned to base. As we had crossed the Arctic Circle near the Lofoten Islands on January 1 1943 I qualified for my Bluenose certificate, which was signed by Lieutenant Commander Peter Agnew on behalf of the Captain.

Our next assignment was to pick up a convoy in Loch Ewe in the Minches and to assemble with a convoy at Sedjesfiord on the east coast of Iceland. This was a very deep fiord where the granite cliffs came down sheer into the sea and so ships could moor up alongside. Of course we had destroyers with us, because the whole of the sea area south of Iceland, and east to Murmansk, was patrolled by U-Boats, and in some places they were hunting in packs. So escort vessels with depth charges were necessary at convoy speeds, at other times when we were cruising at around 30 knots we could avoid torpedos. I remember during one middle watch on the way to Russia we had a U-Boat steaming on the surface, no doubt charging their batteries, only about a mile astern of us. Through my binoculars I could see the Captain on the conning tower quite clearly in the moonlight. When I asked why we did not sink him, I was told the resulting gunfire flash would give away our position to another U-Boat in the pack ahead of us. (What I did not know at the time was that Bletchley Park had their coding machine and could tell the positions of the U-Boats.) Anyway that seemed a good enough reason at the time not to fire. When dawn came up she had disappeared.

After leaving Sedjesfiord, we zigzagged our way towards Murmansk behind the convoy, as protection against the German Cruisers and Battleships, with our own Battleships behind until we were off the North Cape of Norway. We kept as far north as possible past Jan Mayen and Bear Islands to avoid air attack. The cold was terrible up there, there was always a sea running, and so as the spray came aboard and then froze on our guard rails, and more seriously our forward eight-inch guns. So the crew had to go out in droves for twenty minutes each gang to hammer the ice off the guns and forecastle, a very unpleasant task. I remember that during one middle watch, I was on my half hour rest in the shelter behind the air defence position, and it was so cold even in Arctic clothing that I felt like going to sleep and not waking up. This was a classic example of hypothermia, however the others kept me going. Perhaps the bonus of being up there was that we were issued with an extra tot of rum during the dog watches to keep our spirits up.

As we drew away from Iceland and started to go outside the range of the RAF Sunderland Flying Boats, which did such amazing service during the war in helping the Navy to spot U-Boats, and indeed destroying them, we signalled with regret to the last one to leave us. After that normally previous convoys had no air cover until within range of Murmansk, this was because Aircraft Carriers were in short supply due to sinkings, most notably the loss of HMS *Glorious* in Norwegian waters and the *Ark Royal* elsewhere. However some of the Merchant ships with us were fitted with steam catapults on their forecastles and Hurricane fighters with RAF pilots. When they had done battle with the Germans these chaps had to land their planes alongside a Destroyer and be hauled up a scrambling net, the plane having been written off. They were extremely brave men and I am glad to say got an automatic DFC.

Off the North Cape the expected air attacks started with an attack by Stuka dive bombers, one of which was soon shot down. However one got through and managed to drop his bomb a foot or two away from where I was sitting and thankfully slithered down our ship's side bursting on our Armour plating belt further amidships, as we were doing 32 knots at the time. We cheered however as the portside four-inch gun battery shot him down as he levelled out the other side of the ship.

Next came the most significant event: we were attacked by a squadron of Heinkel-111 torpedo-carrying bombers again on the starboard side. The Gunnery Officer gave what must have been one of the first ever such orders in the Royal Navy 'standby to fire one eight-inch broadside to starboard BY RADAR'. The planes continued to carry on towards the ship on the steady course which torpedo attacks require, and suddenly there was the usual huge blast of our guns and 8 eight-inch anti-aircraft shells exploded a nautical mile (2000yds) from the ship. There was a vast explosion and fire in the sky, and a moment of silence before all of us on deck throughout the ship started cheering, and indeed irrespective of rank hugging each other as survivors of what otherwise might have been a deadly attack. This was the result achieved by the new Radar fitted in Liverpool (and as my story unfolds later on I was to find out its technology two years later in my Naval career), so Admiral Sir Percy Noble's comments about us being designed to give the Germans up there a bloody nose had come true. I would imagine that the German Airforce up there were perturbed to say the least, and it seems that these losses led to their withdrawal thereafter from that posting since they then realized that we had a new weapon. In fact after that convoy these attacks started to cease and except for surface vessels and U-Boat attacks, which went on to the end of the convoys, that was it as far as the German Airforce was concerned.

We and our Squadron of two other Cruisers, the *Berwick* and the *Glasgow*, were welcomed into the Kola Bay Naval Base by a Russian Destroyer escort, the merchant ships proceeded on to Murmansk itself to dock and unload their precious cargos, mostly of tanks, aircraft and ammunition.

Maybe things had changed, but contrary to some reports the Russian Naval and Military authorities were welcoming to us ordinary sailors at least, and we were given a good party in the Barracks ashore where, to my delight we 'scholled' a lot of Vodka before returning aboard. I have been a fan of it ever since! It was significant that all the Russian ranks mixed together on such occasions, though I would hazard a guess that they were short like us of interpreters! However on our ship, except for talking on duty, we seldom conversed or met, at least other than at prayers or at ship's concerts, except for those employed in the Wardroom, Gunroom, or Warrant Officer's Messes. This, I am sure, was a pity, because so many of us ordinary sailors had at the lowest level something to contribute to the understanding of our very much admired superiors, a lesson I that have carried throughout my later life. Contrary to much popular opinion the ordinary men in the Royal Navy tended to be hand picked, as even during the Second World War they only recruited volunteers, and as their ships were full of engineering technology by then, they had to be up to it. So we had many craftsmen amongst us whom it was worth learning from, (as an artist now I still learn from craftsmen), and whilst the different ranks, and age groups therefore, had, quite properly, their own Messdecks to live and socialize in, it always seemed to me a pity that we did not mix occasionally to exchange ideas. I was to find in later life that an occasional social function in the shipbuilding yard that I ran, until the Government closed it down by imposing a special tax 17% more than the rate for anything else, was helped to succeed to a great extent by the help and advice of the craftsmen involved.

When the ships had unloaded we left with the convoy returning to the UK, having embarked some of the wounded crew members from the Destroyer *Onslow* which had been hit during the action in which the Cruisers *Sheffield* and *Jamaica* were involved, and which I have previously referred to. We happened to have a fine

HMS Kent entering Kola Bay near Murmansk – 1943

Sick Bay on board, though since they had been put ashore after the action, they had recovered to a certain extent and were fit enough to stand the voyage home. I am glad to say that as a result no doubt of the German Airforce losses in that theatre of operations we had only the U-Boats to contend with on the way back.

Soon after completing these operations Admiral Sir Bruce Fraser took over from Admiral Tovey as CinC in the new Battleship *Duke of York*, and the *King George V* of the same class left the Home Fleet to go eastwards. Admiral Tovey became CinC of the Nore Command. Admiral Fraser eventually came aboard us and gave us an inspiring address, he struck us as an unusually good leader and gave us confidence that we would win through. After doing a 'White' patrol against surface Raiders such as the *Tirpitz* between Iceland and Greenland where we met a violent storm of hurricane force strength, we were given a minor refit in Glasgow and two week's leave each watch. As I had been in the service for about a year, and had passed all the tests on board to qualify, I was on the recommendation of the Officers of our Division promoted to Able Seaman before going on leave. This was a distinction equal to Lance Corporal in the Army, and one which I was to enjoy for the next year or two. It meant that my pay would be an extra one shilling a day, namely two shillings and sixpence, otherwise all found.

It was a great relief to get home after several months at sea, though my father was impatient still with my lack of progress towards Commissioned rank. So that my hard earned promotion to the rank that I felt justly proud of was not graciously welcomed, even though I had been told that a place in the RNVR Officers' training school would be forthcoming in due course. However he accepted that as an Ordinary Seaman I had done my duty. What I did not anticipate was that word had got around in the village of my birth that I had been on Russian Convoy, as a result when I went into the village pubs I got a tremendous welcome, and drinks on the house in two of them.

At the end of my leave, I took the local train from Bredon up to Birmingham New Street where I changed on to the night express to Glasgow, the first scheduled stop being Wolverhampton.

In the compartment were several servicemen including a Sergeant Major, who when the train pulled up picked up his case and opening the door of the carriage jumped down onto what appeared to be in the wartime blackout the edge of a platform. He had left the door open behind him, and as I was next to it I got up to shut it. The train then suddenly started to move, which seemed strange as I could not hear the usual noise and whistles of a station, so I lowered the window and looked out. To my astonishment I could see the faint glow of lights below, which seemed to indicate that we had stopped on a bridge or something of the sort. Thereupon I pulled the communication cord above the door, as it seemed that the Sergeant Major might have had an accident. I conferred with the other two servicemen in the compartment, both soldiers, and we decided on looking out, having opened our carriage door fully so that the Guard would see us, to climb down onto the track and investigate.

We realized immediately that in fact the train had stopped on a high viaduct, which was somewhere outside Wolverhampton Station. We all ran back towards the rear of the train where we met an irate Guard who wanted to know what the devil we were doing stopping his Express. We explained what seemed to have happened, and he then helped us to investigate with his lamp. Some way back along the viaduct we heard groans and sure enough down below we could see a body slumped on the ground. The Guard then ordered us to get back in the train, as he would arrange to contact the nearest signal box so as to deal with the problem when the train arrived at Wolverhampton, where he said we would be interviewed. When the communication cord, of which there seemed to be a large amount hanging down in our compartment, had been reset, the train started off again, and we were duly interviewed by two detectives in the train before it proceeded northwards. Thankfully the police agreed to give us a note to hand in at the other end to explain the delay caused to our return from leave.

Some weeks later I was asked to attend Commander's report (a form of muster) and received a commendation for my action in helping to save the Sergeant Major's life, which I was pleased about. That I thought was the end of story. But life is full of the most extraordinary coincidences, and there was to be one in the sequence to this event. Just over two years later I was travelling home from Portsmouth in naval uniform having been discharged from the Royal Navy in April 1946 after the end of the war. When waiting for my train home from Paddington, I went into the station buffet on platform one, and sat down with a coffee in one of the few seats available. The man sitting opposite me looked closely at me, and said I am a Detective Inspector from Wolverhampton, and I think that I recognize you as the sailor I interviewed on a train going to Glasgow about two years ago about a soldier falling off a viaduct there. This was quite amazing, and I then heard the outcome in full. The Sergeant Major, as I knew, had survived, but apparently he had broken all his limbs in the fall. However as he fell his bag went underneath him, thus protecting his body from injury, and after a long time in hospital he was released back into the Army for a role in training. Although I was several hours late rejoining my ship, I told him that his note had let me off! He was interested to hear about some of my experiences thereafter before our train arrived.

Perhaps more interesting than all of this is to relate the experiences we had during the two weeks we had on duty watch in Glasgow. There is no doubt in my mind, due to my later experiences, as you will hear, that Glasgow was the most generous and appreciative city in the country to members of HM Forces during the Second World War, and this is my chance to give thanks. My uncle, who was stationed there in the Army as a Major, agreed with me on this. The Glasgow people gave us free admittance to dance halls cinemas and so on, they could not have done more for us as service personnel. There were requests to us on board ship every day to attend all sorts of things. I was signed to attend a wedding of a Royal Navy sailor from another ship, as I thought that I might learn something of the slums of the notorious part of the city in which it was held. This was very interesting as the people living in these awful slum high-rise flats were in fact no different from the rest of us. They were merely deprived people like we have today. I felt sorry for them, as I do now. Our budding civil servants, who tip straight out of universities, have never understood that at the lowest level of our society the privacy and surroundings of people in general matter. Today there are many people who cannot even afford a house, let alone rent one, and so they have to live in a caravan, where the authorities, lawyers, and police pursue them with some relish, quite disgracefully. I was hopeful that after the War, and all our collective experiences in this country, we might overcome poverty amongst ourselves, a hope not realized because of the structure of our civil administration, which fails us continuously, quite irrespectively of the political party in power.

However to return to the Arctic, I have yet to relate the time that we found ourselves in a 120-knot hurricane in the Denmark Strait between Greenland and Iceland. There had been a hurricane coming up from the Caribbean and this met a Low coming off Labrador which intensified it. The storm started with a flattened sea with spume coming off it. Then followed what was a gale with vast seas of not less than 80 ft. An Able Seaman of many years' experience told me whilst standing on the after part of the bridge that we needed to say our prayers as he was sure that we could not last through it. The ship was heading into the sea at a speed of two knots, but the engines were producing a speed of 22 knots. I owe my life to the Captain who in spite of being deluged on the Bridge by these immense waves kept us on course to survive. HMS *Sheffield* which was with us on this occasion lost a triple 6.5-inch turret over the side, and people after the war found this hard to believe. As it was when we came out of the storm there were no guard rails or stanchions left standing on the forecastle, quarter-inch steel mushroom vents were flattened against the armour plating of the forward turret, and with two exceptions all our boats stowed on the upper deck were damaged. Thus we had to have a minor refit. In fact my wife told me to give up on that story as some found it hard to believe.

Nevertheless after the war in 1965 I happened to have a berth for my yacht in the Hamble River near the Bugle Inn at Hamble. I went ashore to have supper there on a Saturday night, and was waiting for my number to be called for a table. There was a Royal Navy Lieutenant standing at the bar, and I got into conversation with him about the Service. Amongst other things I asked him if he was allowed to let me know which ship he was serving on. He

HMS Sheffield 9,100 tons, in the Arctic 1943 – just before losing the for'd gun turret in a force 17 storm off Greenland

said that was no secret and that he was the Officer in charge of HMS *Sheffield*. I asked if this was the Second World War Cruiser *Sheffield*, and he said that she was in 'mothballs' now in Portsmouth Harbour. I told him that she had been in our Cruiser Squadron and had lost the forward 6.5-inch turret over the side in the Denmark Strait. He then asked for a detailed explanation, as nobody could understand it. Apparently there was a brass plate on the turret in memory of the men who had lost their lives on that occasion. I was after that able to believe and tell that story again!

I have previously referred to extraordinary coincidences that can happen in life, but I have to relate that immediately after taking my leave of this Naval Officer, when my table number was called, another one occurred. The pub was very busy, it being a Saturday night, and I was shown to a table where a middle-aged man was sitting with his wife. I apologized for my intervention, whereupon he said: I am glad to welcome you because I heard you mention to that Officer at the bar that you had something to do with HMS *Kent*. He then said that he vaguely remembered me, though I was not in his Division, (one has to explain that with a total of over 700 people on board we did not all know each other). So we had quite an evening together recalling our experiences on that and other occasions; apparently he lived locally in Southampton.

When we rejoined operations we went back to Hafval Fiord in Iceland in company with the *Duke of York* under Admiral Fraser and other ships of the fleet. On a previous occasion when we visited that fiord it was very cold, and there were ice floes about in the water. I had been detailed to repaint a damaged part of the starboard side together with a South African Able Seaman. We had to lower ourselves on the staging down the ship's side by undoing the rope from the stage, and whilst holding both parts together let the rope slide. The South African, as one might expect, felt the cold more than myself, and let the rope slip out of his hands, and as a result we both were thrown into the water, to be rescued by a launch. I must say that my legs started to go completely numb before I was hauled out, it was frightening, and the South African had to be taken ashore to the hospital as he nearly died. He never returned to the ship again. He should never have been given that job in the first place. So Hafval Fiord had unhappy memories from that occasion, and indeed the one that I am about to relate. There we were joined by two American Battleships together with some Cruisers and Destroyers who had come to relieve our hard-pressed Navy in the western Atlantic. This was a great occasion and we were glad meet their crew members and to celebrate in the fleet canteen ashore. When the canteen shut as we made our way down a railway track to our respective liberty boats, some fellows had let go a railway wagon and it came tearing down the track. Fortunately I and also a friend from my ship heard it coming, but an American sailor who was with us did not manage to jump clear and the wagon took his right arm off. Fortunately my friend had been a Policeman in the Metropolitan Police in Civvy Street, and he knew where the pressure point to deal with the loss of blood was. He told me to take the left arm over my shoulder and we frog marched this poor chap who was in a desperate state up to the base hospital. We were told the next day that the Doctors had managed to save him, much to everyone's relief. That must have been the end of his service career. I am glad to say that the American Captain came aboard and we were both sent for and thanked, my friend in particular as without his First Aid knowledge things would no doubt have been very different.

In early April 1943 as part of our patrol of the Denmark Strait we were allowed to anchor for a week in Akureyri Fiord in the very North of Iceland. It was a lovely little snowbound town looking like Switzerland. The American Army were in control ashore and were our very generous hosts. At the start of the week a request was made over the Tannoy for any members of the ship's company who knew how to rig an RN dinghy to report to the Quartermaster's Lobby. I duly reported there. The Chief Petty Officer on duty asked what I was there for. I told him, and he said, 'What, you?' (they always were the same to us non regulars) 'How do you know about RN dinghys?' I then told him that my grandfather had one aboard his yacht before the war. To the surprise of everyone nobody else turned up. So I was ordered to report to the Admiral's Secretary, who in turn ushered me into the Admiral's presence. He was very interested about my grandfather's yacht, which was known to him. He told me to get the boat over the side and rigged, and he would come and join me in about half an hour. I duly got the boat rigged and the Admiral joined me with his fishing gear, and off we sailed from the ship, to join the fleet of boats, which had been already lowered into the water, and manned by the duty upper deck crew.

The fiord was a long one and so there was plenty of room for everyone to fish. This process continued throughout the week, and the fishing was biblical – as fast as lines were cast fish, mostly cod and plaice, were landed in the boats in great quantity, so much so that the entire ship's company were fed for the duration of our stay, and when frozen for about two weeks thereafter. The Admiral was however more interested in fishing selectively for salmon and sea trout with rod and line. He required me to sail the boat, or when there was too much or too little wind to row it. For this type of fishing the noise of an engine, which the other boats had, was not good for the purpose. He caught a lot of fish also, so that his end of the ship was well supplied during our stay in that fiord. The weather was amazingly good for the whole week, and we all enjoyed our stay, not least because of the hospitality out of hours with the Americans ashore. At the end of the week the Admiral thanked me for my help, and added that he had enjoyed our exchange of experiences. I shall always remember him saying to me at the end of it all that Admirals and Able Seamen had a lot in common as neither of them had much to lose. He was a most delightful man to talk to, and had a good sense of humour. After that when I saw him on the Bridge, since by that time I was the Captain's messenger, he used to give me a little wave of acknowledgement, much to the concern of the other Officers on watch, not a matter considered acceptable to strict Naval discipline.

Whilst on this subject of the friendliness of many of our senior Officers, I must break off and mention a couple of tales about our then CinC Admiral Sir Bruce Fraser (later Admiral of the Fleet Lord Fraser of North Cape). I remember the 5000 tons six-inch gun Cruiser HMS *Arethusa* well. She was with us in the fleet in Scapa Flow. Well after the war I joined up in legal practice with a friend of mine in Birmingham called Bill Kentish who like me had served in the Royal Navy. When in the *Arethusa*, he as a Lieutenant RNVR (later Lieutenant Commander RNR) was Officer of the Watch around midnight on a dead calm moonlight night, when an Able Seaman turned up to request permission to bathe off the motor boat's boom. Bill thought the chap was joking and gave permission, whereupon there was a huge splash and the peace of the anchorage was shattered. It so happened that Admiral Sir Bruce Fraser was taking the air on deck before turning in and had witnessed the event. Next morning the Captain of the *Arethusa* received a signal from the flagship to report the name of the Officer of the middle watch the previous night and to send him aboard the flagship to see the CinC. The Captain sent for Bill and expressed his displeasure about what had happened but said that he would leave it to the CinC to deal with, as he hoped harshly, with the matter. Bill Kentish duly appeared before the Admiral in the flagship, and the Admiral asked his Secretary to pour him a gin and tonic. He asked Bill about his background and his life in Civvy Street, and had quite a social conversation. He then asked about the incident the night before, Bill told him that he did not expect the chap really meant it. The Admiral then thanked Bill for coming, and said that the intentions of the men always had to be believed, as he had no doubt now learnt. Bill had to report on the interview to his Captain when he got back, and the Captain was amazed that he had not been disciplined. This shows what a reasonable and good leader Sir Bruce was.

Another well known incident later on after the war happened on Paddington Station when the then Admiral of the Fleet Lord Fraser of North Cape was travelling to Plymouth to inspect the Navy down there. He was by then the First Sea Lord and in full uniform ready for his parade, and was standing on Platform 1 waiting for the Plymouth train. This had been held up because the Cheltenham Spa express had not yet gone out of the platform. Presently an old lady came up to him in haste, and said to him, 'Stationmaster, could you please come and put my luggage on the rack as I cannot manage lifting it.' The Admiral said, 'Certainly, Madam,' and duly obliged her. She then pressed two shillings and sixpence (12.5p) into his hand. He looked at it and said 'that is hardly a good enough tip for a Stationmaster, Madam, is it?' Whereupon she fished in her purse and duly pulled out another half crown. The Admiral then stepped out of the train and was convulsed in laughter with his Staff Officer with him, and related the story to many afterwards. What an amusing man, his sense of humour and lack of pomposity were typical of most Naval Officers, though I did come across some exceptions. After I left the fleet at Scapa Flow he did of course go on to win the decisive Battle of the North Cape, when the German Battleship *Scharnhorst* was sunk.

In May 1943, when we were in Iceland again, I was told that I was to be returned to Chatham Barracks to await drafting to the RNVR Officers' training school at HMS *King Alfred*, Brighton. I was therefore to take passage back to Scapa Flow in the fleet tanker *Blue Ranger* to which I was transferred. The Captain interviewed me before I left together with Lieutenant Henley and they wished me success. So to my surprise Petty Officer Whitlock came to wish me well, and praised my service aboard, so I had evidently passed his bullying type of approach, which shows that if you stand up to such things you win in the end. I also had a moving send off from many messmates. I was not sorry to be leaving the Arctic or the Russian convoys, but otherwise I enjoyed life aboard HMS *Kent*. She was a good and comfortable ship, unlike the next one I was to serve in which was very cramped by comparison.

I was duly transferred to the Fleet tanker and supply ship *Blue Ranger* for passage back to Scapa Flow. She had been refuelling the Aircraft Carrier HMS *Furious* in Hafval Fiord Iceland amongst others, and was still partly loaded with aero spirit, and so she had her own Minesweeper escort. There were several of us Ratings aboard as passengers with a Leading Seaman in charge. We had of course some Naval DEMS Gunners aboard to man the six-inch gun on the stern, with which all such ships were fitted, so as to repel the attacks of surfaced U-Boats. So we had some Naval mates as well as the well paid Merchant Navy crew, who were very good to us.

As we put out to sea, the usual gale in that sea area started, and a Collier (a large tramp steamer) that had been refuelling in Iceland was with us in ballast, so its propeller was more out of the water than in it, which caused the convoy to reduce speed considerably. However us passengers got down to playing a seemingly endless game of fraz, which was in effect a game of Lotto with cards, and depended on the turn of a card by the dealer. It seemed to be to me a much more profitable game than most other gambling card games that I had known. Since there were few if any occasions up in the Arctic to spend one's pay (even cigarettes, which we all smoked then were, only the equivalent of 5p a packet), we Arctic Convoy men were reasonably well off. Therefore we really got down to full time gambling, which was great fun after what we had been through.

However before the day was out our Royal Navy escort had picked up a U-Boat on its Sonar, and then began firing depth charges in order to force it to the surface, if not sink it. Thus an alarm was sounded and all off-duty crew and passengers were ordered into the lifeboats, which were then slung at the ready over the ship's side. This was considered necessary due to the very highly inflammable aero spirit cargo. Imagine sitting as it was getting dark in a open lifeboat in a rising gale. As it was we had been detached from the convoy, which was too slow for a ship designed to steam at 18 knots, and had been ordered to proceed under our own power with one of the escorts. After about two hours being tossed around and frozen, we passengers felt that it was better to face possible death in the warm down below playing cards, so we climbed out of the lifeboat and went about our business of playing cards. After all, us chaps had faced worse problems on our way to Russia than being blown up aboard a tanker! On the next day we were ordered to fall in before the Tanker Captain on the Bridge, and we were told that we would be reported to the Naval Authorities in Scapa Flow, where we were to be landed, as having disobeyed the Captain's orders. I am glad to say that when we disembarked and were interviewed by the Base Commander, we were dismissed with a caution, our service in one of the worst areas of Naval conflict having been taken into account. After landing we were sent over on the ferry to Thurso were we were accommodated until the train left for London the next day. That voyage had made me rich for the first time as I had been very lucky in my gambling aboard the *Blue Ranger*. I was given two weeks leave starting from when our train arrived in London and ordered to report to Chatham Barracks to await drafting to HMS *King Alfred*, the RNVR Officers' training school.

CHAPTER 6

At Chatham and HMS *King Alfred*

I MUST SAY I ENJOYED MY TWO WEEKS leave in a warm climate again, after the privations of the Arctic, in some respects too much perhaps. I caught a train from Paddington to Gloucester, and then changed there for Bredon on the Midland line. When I got out at Bredon, Frank Farbrother the Chief Porter there, whom I knew well, gave me a great welcome and helped me with my kit. As it was after the evening opening time, he invited me to have a drink in the Railway Inn next door to the Station, both of which are now sadly closed. Jack Turner the publican asked me if I had ever tried Scrumpy. I said no, so he said I could have it on the house. I had several glasses, which were good to taste but not otherwise, since I apparently, not having eaten since since breakfast, passed out and Jack had to send for the ARP stretcher party to carry me home with my kit to the Manor House. They put me to bed and left. Next morning, although nursing a hangover I went down to greet my parents. My father happened to be the chief of the village ARP and it suffices to say that he made his extreme displeasure known to me. I promised that I would never drink Scrumpy again, a vow I have kept ever since. He was so angry to start with that I suggested that it might have been better if I had not returned from the Arctic and perished up there, which I had a narrow escape from anyway. His anger then cooled, bless him, and he merely asked for my assurance not to do such a thing again. I think that I can claim to have lived a reasonably sober life since, it was a stupid thing to do on an empty stomach with such pure alcohol; people who drink that have to be used to it!

I remember on that leave meeting Lt Commander John Moore, a Fleet Air Arm pilot, for the first of many occasions. He had been invalided out of the Royal Navy due to a bad crash. He was married to a charming Australian Wren, called Louise, who had

50

been released to look after him, and whom I was in touch with until her recent death. John was a great author, particularly about country life, and remains famous to this day for his books about life around the Bredon Hill area. We both got on immediately and he was very interested to hear about the rigours of the Arctic.

When my much needed leave was over, I duly reported to HMS *Pembroke* (namely Chatham Barracks), and found that I had been immediately posted into the Commodore's Guard, which was a surprise, as I had thought my draft to HMS *King Alfred* was to be immediate. The Commodore's Guard was an elite section of Ratings used to high standards of parade ground drill, and so was not only given a very good Mess and accommodation in the barracks, but also a perhaps deserved esteem. My second day on parade found me as the right hand man, and therefore marker, which seemed a great distinction. We were fallen in to welcome the newly appointed Commodore, and to parade before him at noon and present arms etc accompanied by the usual Band of the Royal Marines. Imagine my surprise when my Ex-skipper Captain Angus Cunninghame Graham DSO turned up as the Commodore. At the end of the parade he did the usual inspection, and spoke to me in his usual quarterdeck style. He was unusually as a Scot one of the only pompous Naval Officers that I came across in the Royal Navy, except for Admiral Sir Geoffrey Leyton. In fact I suppose that due to the closeness of seafaring men, we were more united than the Military in the way we operated. Anyway once again he formally wished me well, and passed on down the line. I can say this, I shall always revere him as having been a damned fine Skipper.

After two or three weeks of really enjoyable formal parading in the Commodore's Guard (since I had obtained my Certificate A at Eton, and therefore an Officer qualification in the Army) I was duly drafted to the RNVR Officer's training school, much to my father's delight!

We were given some very comfortable private digs in Hove to start with in a boarding house, with a very nice landlady. This was for the two weeks while at Mowden in Hove the Naval Training Officers sorted out our degree of competence by various tests, which were to establish how high in the system we should start. This was good because after my very extended seatime I was enabled to start at a higher level. During my time I came across a Leading Wren, Diana Rigg, who became a friend of mine until some time after the war, and we corresponded, but although we visited each other's homes it came to nothing, just one of my failed romances.

After this period we moved up to Lancing College. This was a splendid Victorian Public School which had been evacuated and taken over by the Admiralty for the period of the War. Queen Victoria had taken an interest in its foundation and the Chapel had been modelled on Eton College Chapel, so as a practising Christian I felt at home so to speak, even masquerading as a member of the Church of Scotland! This was even the more so because the Naval Chaplain in charge at Lancing was the Reverend Douglas Graham, who as a Master and Curate of Eton College, had not only taught me, but instructed me for Confirmation. He was glad to see me and hear about my time at Cambridge and my adventures on the Russian Convoy. I have already referred to at least one of several coincidences in my life, and at this stage I must mention another. After the war when I got married I went to live in Great Comberton near Pershore in Worcestershire, and I served for seven years as a Churchwarden there, mostly under a saint of a Rector, who apart from having been a missionary in South America, had been a Destroyer Captain in the First World War. His name was Ernest Panter, and he told me that the Headmaster of Dean Close School in Cheltenham was coming to take Evensong one Sunday night, and I was to attend upon him, as he would not be there, and my fellow Churchwarden would be away also. The Church was well attended in those days, and at six thirty there was no sign of a Clergyman. A lot of people will not know that if a priest does not turn up for an ordinary service, other than Communion, then the Churchwardens, through their sworn authority, are authorized to hold a service without certain rites. Accordingly I asked the organist to extend the voluntary for five minutes, and then gave out the number of the first hymn, whereupon the vestry door opened and there standing before me to my surprise was the Reverend Douglas Graham. You can imagine my relief, and he came home with me after the Service, and we caught up with our respective lives once again. Amazing is it not!

At Lancing College we were well taught in the art of navigation, which was of great benefit to me after the war when I went Ocean Racing. Signals were the other study of importance, and I have to admit that I found the Morse Code side of these difficult. However the several weeks that we stayed there were enjoyable, and the place quite comfortable.

We were then transferred to a brand new Leisure Centre in Brighton itself for the final passing out procedures and interviews. I was Officer of the Day at the final parade of our draft. After that I was interviewed by the Admiralty Board, and told that I had failed the signals part of the exam and was to be drafted back to sea to polish up my signals. I was given a week's leave and told to report back to Chatham, which I did. However my leave was upset a bit, as my father was furious at my failure to attain Officer status. So I arrived back in Chatham once more but almost immediately they found me a draft to a Corvette at Harwich called HMS *Puffin*, and so a new chapter began.

CHAPTER 7

HMS *Puffin* and the east coast convoys

HMS *PUFFIN* WAS PART OF the flotilla of Destroyers, Corvettes, and Minesweepers based at Parkeston Quay Harwich. This base was on a railway terminus for ferries to the Continent, which was handy when we got some leave. The base was the other side of the estuary from HMS *Ganges* where I did my initial training, so when I was the morning watch before breakfast, I had sight of the chaps learning to climb the famous mast there.

The *Puffin* was originally commissioned in 1932 as a Coastal patrol and fishery protection vessel, and incidentally the Petty Officer Boatswain and the ship's Cook had been with her since then, which I think was quite a record. Her dimensions were displacement 530 tons, length 243ft, beam 26.5ft, and draft 6ft. Speed was 22 knots. The armament consisted of a single four-inch gun on the forecastle, 2 double-barrelled machine guns to starboard and port of the Bridge, one Oerliken gun and two single-barrelled machine guns both sides amidships, two four-barrelled Vickers guns (pom-poms) on both sides aft, and finally a Vickers machine gun on the quarterdeck. Right aft we carried two racks full of depth charges, and finally and most important Radar and Asdic (later called Sonar, as I suppose it rhymed with Radar!). She had two boiler rooms, and was driven by two lovely little Parsons steam turbines giving her 3600 horsepower, in a grand little engine room. Her shape was like that of a miniature Destroyer, a handsome little ship. The crew consisted of five Officers and 65 Other Ranks.

Soon after joining I was interviewed by the Captain who was a Lieutenant Commander RNZVR, (I do wish that I could now recall his name, because he turned out to be one of those very nice New Zealanders, and an excellent Skipper. He had in fact been a keen yachtsman before the war), who questioned me on why I had been drafted aboard to learn signals, as it seemed to him rather unusual. However having explained the circumstances, he was most understanding, and said that he would ask the Leading

HMS Puffin 530 tons – Corvette – built 1932, Chief Quartermaster, the Artist

55

Signalman to train me whenever there was an opportunity, though this might be rather seldom as the ship's company was being kept very busy due to the shortage of escort vessels, so many having been sunk.

I was in fact to spend just over the next six months aboard the good ship *Puffin* (her nickname was Blowing), this was longer than I had expected, but was put down to shortage of manpower. *Puffin* was a Seabird class Corvette (called by some a member of the duck class, I suppose with perhaps justification as other ships in our 1st Corvette Flotilla were called *Mallard, Widgeon, Sheldrake,* and *Kittiwake*). Our mooring buoys were in a straight line, outside those of the Destroyers, and parallel to Parkeston Quay in the River Stour. Our duties along with the Destroyers (which were both V&W class and Hunt Class ships) were to protect the East Coast convoys running between the Thames, Humber, and ports further north. The sea area between the Thames and Wash was protected on the outside, except for access gaps, by our own minefields at a depth of about three fathoms. So the convoys sailed between these, which were marked by coded buoys, and the shore, and this gave them an element of protection. Also we had to in turn, in company with some of the motor torpedo boats from Felixstowe, to patrol against the German E-Boats, which were in the habit of shifting the mining ground buoys on a frequent basis, in order to mine the convoys with our own mines. We had also to deal with the hazard of Magnetic mines, on occasion, though most of this work was dealt with by our fleet of Trawler Minesweepers, who thankfully were most efficient in carrying it out.

Except for the air attacks by Dorniers mostly, and the occasional U-Boat attack in the deeper parts up north, as of course the area off most of East Anglia is fairly shallow, the convoys got through with only a few losses. Midget Submarines, which operated in good weather, and the E-Boats, which likewise needed reasonable weather, were the menace there. Generally speaking we did a convoy and then following that an E-boat patrol.

As I had qualified as an Able Seaman gunner aboard the *Kent*, I was detailed to man the twin Lewis machine gun on the starboard side of the Bridge during the call to Action Stations. When dealing with the E-Boats, which generally occurred in the dark under star shell, my specific orders were to rake the crew on deck with fire, leaving the other guns to sink the vessel. This worked well and I had quite a lot of success.

On one occasion though the Germans nearly had me in the bag. Our patrol, consisting of three MTBs steaming at our full speed of twenty two knots, sure enough found the enemy shifting one of the mining buoys, whereupon the MTBs ahead of us opened up to their full speed, then encircled the enemy and retreated behind us. Whereupon we opened fire at close range with our 4-inch gun, and the rest of our armament, the enemy still closing, not realizing that we had greater fire power than the MTBs. The E-Boat came strait at us at full speed, and our 4-inch crew got him as he came round broadside on to us, and he blew up with a almighty flash only around 100 ft from us. I had my eyebrows taken off by the explosion. The 4-inch gun's crew were cheering, and then one of my mates was sent down from the Bridge to see if I was alright. I had not realized that my eyebrows were missing at the time. He said 'Are you OK, Lofty?' to which I replied, ' Yes why do you ask?', and he said, 'Well, take a look behind you and you will see.' The steel plating on side of the Bridge in line with my gun, and therefore myself, was lined with the dents of shell bursts from the Oerliken gun of the E-Boat: so that was another one of my close escapes!

I only intend to relate the incidents out of the ordinary. There are some that may be interesting. One of these was the occasion when the Officer's Steward (Known as a 'Jack Dusty') who was on his way up to the Bridge just before lunch, while I as Chief Quartermaster had taken over the ship's helm from the Coxswain who was down below supervising the rum issue, was swept overboard in gale conditions. Everyone having to go above deck at sea was required to wear a lifejacket, so Jack Dusty floated off astern having mercifully missed the propellers. On the shout 'Man Overboard!' we rang down 'Stop Engines', and then the Captain stated that I would now, as a future Officer of the Watch, learn how to do a Robinson's turn to enable the ship to weather down upon a man to effect a rescue. He stated that we had to keep calm and steam on for three ship's lengths before turning to come on the weather side of the casualty very slowly, then stop engines, and effect rescue. This he carried out brilliantly, but then the Almighty intervened, and a huge wave came over the stern in just the right place, and the Jack Dusty landed on the quarterdeck, shook himself, and went down below to shower and change. He then went down to the Wardroom to serve the Officers' lunch. Men had grit in those days, no counselling being necessary!

As I had already been through the RNVR Officer's training course, the Captain had given me some unusual privileges for an Able Seaman, the main one being that he appointed me Chief Quartermaster. This, apart from being on the helm and in charge of the chaps on the engine room telegraphs, involved being in charge of the Quartermaster's lobby at the entrance to the Wardroom, and with the other duty Quartermasters, maintaining the Ship's Log under the instructions of the duty Officer of the Watch. In addition we had to call the attention of the crew to the various orders of the day over the Tannoy system. We were also responsible for use of a boatswain's pipe to salute other Naval vessels, and to call the ship's Company to attention. I enjoyed the job, and still have my Boatswain's Pipe as a memento.

Having possibly bored you with all this detail, I will now relate how I was unusually allowed, as an Able Seaman, to take the ship up into the Fish Dock in Hull Docks by the Captain. He of course knew that I had been instructed and examined in ship handing, which I had passed in, at HMS *King Alfred*. So he decided to give me a bit of practice, and let me give all of the helm and telegraph orders to bring the ship in through the lock and to dock alongside. He stated that any wrong order he would immediately countermand. I am glad to say that no such orders had to be given, and indeed he congratulated me at the end of it. An unusual distinction for an Able Seaman perhaps!

Apart from the skirmishes to be expected from the enemy, particularly E-Boats, there were one or two more incidents of a more amusing nature to relate. Firstly there was the occasion when one Sunday morning we left Harwich to pick up a convoy. As we left the mooring, and salutes to other ships were made, the duty crew fallen in on deck were dismissed, and then sea duty men were piped to close up. This required them to check their respective equipment ready for action stations being called. The four-inch gun's crew asked the Gunnery Officer if he wanted the gun loaded, and he said yes. Our ordinance artificer Able Seaman Gunner Adams came along later to check the four-inch gun firing mechanism. He failed to notice from checking the indicator that the gun was loaded, and as he usually did checked the firing mechanism. As the ship was turning at the time, and the gun was trained fore and aft, the shell that we fired as a result went at a low level straight over the centre of Harwich Town, narrowly missing the church tower. It then landed over a mile beyond the town, and we could see it explode as it hit the water, since it had a sensitive fuse, right alongside the ex P&A Campbell paddle steamer, then HMS *Lorna Doone*, which had been requisitioned as a Minesweeper. Then followed frantic signalling from the paddle wagon, which was enjoying a Sunday rest at anchor, by Aldis lamp, telling us that she was not an enemy ship! It was a near thing for her as I could see her rocking to and fro as a result of the explosion, however she escaped damage. Gunner Adams was taken off the ship when we returned to Harwich and returned to Chatham for Court Martial. We never heard of him again, this was a pity because he had become a friend of mine and was so nice.

Another such incident was when we had returned from a convoy up north, we ran into thick bank of fog off the Cork Lightship just about two miles outside Harwich. We had to anchor there for about 24 hours to let it clear, as our Radar at the time was of the range and bearing type, the PPI type scanner having only just been produced. So it was not safe to proceed. However the engineers reported that we were running out of fuel oil as we had been on a long convoy run, and of course the ship's lighting etc depended on it.

So the Captain had no alternative other than to weigh anchor, and proceed up river into the harbour and anchorage where the oil tanker was moored. The ship proceeded at a dead slow pace, with two lookouts on the bow. Then dead ahead suddenly appeared an RAF balloon barrage barge at anchor, which we had a slight collision with. This was known to be on the Felixstowe side of the estuary so we altered course to West, then not long afterwards there was a shout from the lookouts, and a crunching noise followed as we ran aground. Nobody on board knew where we were then, and as the tide was falling we stuck fast. So the ship's company went to lunch, and whilst we were drawing our tot of rum, a chart was passed around for us to put our money on where we were. Naturally neither the Captain nor Navigating Officer took part, as they were liable to a Court Martial procedure. The winner of the sweep was the Boatswain, he had been on board so long he could smell out our position, we thought. However whilst waiting for lunch, I happened to look out of our porthole, and there was a man standing next to the ship on the beach. He enquired whether we needed help, I laughed, and said that it looked like it, but he had better ask the Chiefs up top, and enquired where we were. He said that we were on the Harwich foreshore just below and in line with the church. The ship refloated itself later that afternoon, and as the fog had lifted quite a bit, we proceeded alongside the tanker.

The next drama was then to occur as we took on oil. Leading Stoker Douglas was down in the Petty Officers' Mess, which was above one of the oil bunkers, and had been given the responsibility for dipping the tank to warn when it was nearly full. He had apparently picked up a magazine down there and was reading it, having assumed that as the tank was nearly empty it would take some time to fill. He was wrong because suddenly the dipping hole in the deck of the Mess exploded with a fountain of thick crude oil, which flooded the Petty Officers' Mess, and, poor chaps, ruined a lot of their kit, as well as their surroundings which had to be replaced. In fact after that the ship was sent to Sheerness for examination in dry dock due to the grounding, and the Petty Officers' Mess was reconditioned, so we got a bit of unexpected leave from all of this. Our Stoker friend paid the ultimate price and was returned to Chatham for Court Martial so that was the last that we saw of him, though I must say he had really asked for trouble, as neglect of duty in the Service was a very serious matter.

Another incident that I recall when I was on duty as Chief Quartermaster one day in harbour after lunch, or Hands' Dinner as it was termed in the forecastle, was when the Captain asked to pipe for the motor boat's crew, as he wanted to go ashore. I duly did this and the crew appeared on deck. Presently the Leading

Seaman Motor Boat Coxswain in charge turned up in the lobby, and reported to me that the motorboat, which had been secured on its boom, had been blown under the gash chute and was full of the lunchtime swill. He said it would take sometime to clear up, would I therefore ask the Captain to wait whilst this was done. I went down and reported this to the Captain who was very far from pleased, and asked if this had occurred on my watch, and I was glad to tell him that I had only just relieved the duty Quartermaster, so he sent for my predecessor, and gave him a dressing down, as one of the duties of Quartermasters in harbour was to keep an eye on the ship's boats whilst they were afloat. He then told me that he was not going to wait, and I was to pipe for the duty watch to man the whaler. That apparently caused a stir down below! Anyhow he went and inspected the motorboat with me, and was not at all pleased. He was then rowed ashore in the whaler. A written order followed the next day, quite rightly ordering men ditching the gash to first look to see that the motorboat was clear of it.

When you consider that except for the Chief Engineer, who was a Commissioned Warrant Officer, the Boatswain, and the Ship's Cook, and one of the Officers who was from the Royal Naval Reserve, all of the rest of the ship's Company were RNVR and therefore wartime Sailors, these incidents were relatively few. It is a tribute to the thoroughness of the Naval training establishments even in wartime. I forgot to relate that before I left Chatham to join the *Puffin* I was given a brief cooking course, since she was what was known as a canteen messing ship, where in rotation you were cook of your Mess for the day, and so you had to use the ingredients supplied to advantage, or else your Mess did not get fed properly. This detail illustrates that training was never neglected.

On one occasion we were having a boiler clean moored alongside Parkeston Quay, which was always welcome because the Off Duty Watch got some leave, in this case one week each Watch. When I was on Duty Watch, we were down below playing cards, when suddenly the ship started to roll even though it was dead calm, and we could hear one of our mooring wires parting. The old hands said that must be Bernard coming in. Anyhow I went up on deck and there was the Captain D of the Destroyer Flotilla, no less than Commander Bernard Jasper De St

Croix DSO and Bar DSC and Bar on the Bridge of his Destroyer. He was one of our war heroes, and indeed later on after the war a hero of the famous Yangtze Incident in China. He was great, I heard him order full astern both, as he approached his berth specially reserved for him on the quay. He then stated 'over to you Number One' to his First Lieutenant, dismounted from the Bridge, landed on the quay where his MG was already parked for him, and roared off. He had been tracked entering the harbour at about twenty knots! I came across him again, as the Commander of HMS *Collingwood* just before I left the Navy. He was a great character.

I think that I have related most of the incidents that happened that will be of interest to the reader. It only remains for me to pay tribute to my comrades the Officers and Men of the good ship *Puffin*, who enabled us all to survive through the hazards of the East Coast battle during my months on board. The war in that sea area was no less of a challenge to the many Naval and Merchant Seamen involved than the Russian Convoys, except that the conditions in the Arctic were unbelievably cold, and immersion in the sea for three minutes meant almost certain death due to hypothermia. Added to which fortunately due to Radar on shore by 1943 the previously dreadful air attacks had become infrequent. From then onwards undoubtedly the E-Boats with their frequent attacks on shipping from Rotterdam and other bases were the menace.

After seven months aboard the *Puffin* I was recalled by Chatham, and departed from that great ship's company with some regret. Though I heard thereafter that apart from taking part in the D–Day landings, she had rammed a German midget submarine and sunk it. However her bow was badly damaged, and although she made dry dock in Sheerness under her own steam, as it was now Spring 1945 and the war was drawing fast to a close, the Admiralty decided to scrap her, sadly. She was a lovely little vessel.

Before this chapter closes, I must comment on my life aboard below decks. Many years after the War in the seventies, a Commander friend of mine in the Royal Yacht Squadron asked me whether it was very rough living in the Forecastle of HM ships. I replied that it depended on the ship. In a Cruiser it was all right other in exceptional conditions, but in the Corvette that I served in, it was indeed rough in heavy weather, but in that instance we were paid a bit extra 'hard lines money'. He then said that he did not mean rough in that sense, but in the sense of the undoubtedly sturdy men living there. I replied that due to their good education in those days, and the fine discipline of the service, as well as the fact that they were all volunteers, and many of them craftsmen, they were good people to live with, and indeed admire. Furthermore due to the training of the Officers, which I had at HMS *King Alfred* been made aware of, the forecastle hands were very well looked after by them, to the extent that I would rate the Navy as a welfare society, and their concern for our wellbeing was a matter I would always remember. It was a point that Lord Nelson made clear in his time, that if the Officers looked after the men and their concerns, and families, then they could be relied on to give good service, and most important win battles. Of course at *King Alfred* we were made to study Nelson, and indeed were examined on his history, as like Wellington and the Army, they were both founders of the service life concept.

After serving on one of the most comfortable class of Cruisers ever built, I have to admit that HMS *Puffin* was more of a Spartan existence. But as I have related we were paid a bit more because of this so there is no complaint. For instance instead of having a recreation room on board, we had to generally play tombola on the main deck. But here I must tell you something rather amusing. We had a few Durham miners serving aboard, and they provided an excellent team of Gunners for the Vickers guns. They were interesting men of great fortitude, as perhaps one might expect, when you consider the great reputation of the Durham Light Infantry. I had some of them in my mess, and they were good fun, always jolly in a difficult situation. They however caused a certain problem for the ship, as we seemed to be constantly short of fresh water. The reason for this was that these chaps were forever having to have showers as a matter of normal habit. So on the anchorage we were asked to have a saltwater shower on deck before having a quick finish off under the shower inside. I was dancing one evening at Dovercourt where the Wrens were stationed, with one of the very attractive Wrens from there, when she revealed that, as a Signaller on the Admiral's staff, she had, through the signalling telescope, admired my nude body whilst taking a saltwater shower on deck in the *Puffin*. Needless to say she became a friend after that but even so I never took a shower on deck again. Actually we could easily have got a quick one ashore. One thing worth recording was the huge support that the WRNS gave us during the war, other than what might be looked upon as natural causes! The Harwich Naval base was almost entirely run by these wonderful women; as far as I know, except for the Rear Admiral in Command, the Commander of the Base, the Signals Officer, the Chief Signals Petty Officer, and the Master of Arms, the base was run by the WRNS. Frankly we were very short of manpower by then, and indeed the motor launches between us and Felixstowe were very ably manned by Wrens.

It was with regret that I had to leave the good ship *Puffin*, to whom I had become much attached, as I had some good shipmates aboard. I was moved very much by their good wishes, and send off.

CHAPTER 8

Life ashore as a radar engineer

I RETURNED TO CHATHAM early in 1944 to be drafted immediately to a training base at Alsager near Stoke on Trent, were I found myself detailed off to do Combined Forces Training, which by that time had become pre-training for RNVR Officers attending HMS *King Alfred*. I was put through a Commando course, I suppose as a pre-requisite for D- Day, which evidently was planned by then. I must say that, even though we were put through the gym prior to doing the course, I only just survived it after about 18 months at sea. At the end we were interviewed by an Admiralty Board prior to being selected to attend *King Alfred*; the goal posts had been changed!

The fact that there was more scrutiny of Candidates for Officer Training in fact worked in my favour, because my records with the Admiralty had evidently come under close examination. I was to learn later on that my records had been marked as unpredictable, as I was wrongly suspected of throwing a bucket of gash over Commander Peter Agnew in the dry dock in Birkenhead. Thus once again I was interviewed in a way that gave me the impression that there was something odd about me. However that fact, whether true or not, turned out to help make my future. The Chairman of the Board, a Rear Admiral, said that my records had been re-examined, and it seemed that as I had taken the Sciences at a high level when entering Cambridge, I might be more suitably employed in the Navy in the Radar division with a view after training to becoming an Electrical Officer. He asked if I would like therefore to be transferred to the Radar division rather than going through *King Alfred* again. Without any hesitation I agreed to be transferred, since I had always fancied a career in Engineering rather than the Law.

Thereupon I was transferred back to Chatham briefly to start studying electrics prior to going to the Northampton Polytechnic in Islington. The V1s had started to arrive in Chatham by that time, and the guns protecting the base and dockyard kept trying to bring them down, without much success, which disturbed us a bit, but the civilian population had the worst of it, as if brought down these terrible weapons generally landed on them.

I was duly drafted to The Northampton Polytechnic Institute in Islington London with two others from Chatham. We were then billeted in an evacuated school in Highbury Road, Islington. It was just up the road from the Polytechnic, and the famous Angel at Islington. Our studies at the Polytechnic had not got very far before the Doodle Bugs caught up with us.

One night we were asleep in our school building when one landed with a huge explosion less than 100 yards away. Our windows were blown out, and the damage just around the corner from us was dreadful. These missiles caused huge lateral damage wherever they were dropped, and therefore they killed a lot of people. Anyway we immediately volunteered to help the local ARP, Police and rescue services. The Polytechnic gave us leave of absence for the purpose. Rescuing those poor people trapped in their houses and giving comfort to the dying once again was not a pleasant task. I became much more aware of the amazing dedication of our national rescue services in performing such tasks, on a daily basis, and remain so to this day.

Later on in the evening, when all the rescue work had been completed, the team from our billet went down to the local pub not far from the back of our school for a drink after supper. Our efforts had been made known by the locals ahead of us in the pub. On arrival at the pub, we were greeted as saviours, and treated to all of our drinks on the house. All of the rest of the time amongst the people there we were met with great kindness.

By that time it was obvious that London was to sustain a concerted attack similar to the blitz, so whilst at the Polytechnic we had to take our turn during the working hours to man the observation post on the roof of the building. If a Doodle Bug was seen to be heading our way we would sound an alarm for the rest of the trainees and staff to take cover. I am glad to say that the building survived as nothing landed close to it. However I happened to be on watch on day when the Goods Yard at St Pancras Station was hit. To give some idea of the strength of these weapons, there were goods wagons flying high in the air well above the height of the station roof.

I passed the exams at the end of the course, better than expected, and was promoted to Leading Seaman, and drafted to the Portsmouth Command at HMS *Victory*. I must say that it was better down there out of the way of the Doodle Bug menace. In those days Portsmouth Barracks and Dockyard were all under the name of HMS *Victory*, the headquarters of which were the famous ship itself. The barracks now are known under the name of HMS *Nelson*, which when I was serving was the name of our mightiest Battleship still afloat.

From Portsmouth, in which command was situated the Radar Headquarters of the Royal Navy at that time at HMS *Collingwood*, Fareham, hence my transfer from Chatham, I was almost immediately drafted to a Radar division at Aberdeen University, where I was still in digs at the time of the D-Day landings. I naturally enjoyed the University and its surroundings whilst I was there. Then I was sent to the Technical College at Glasgow, and was housed in the Naval Base there while I was studied the circuitry of the very latest forms of Radar equipment.

Glasgow was known to be one of the most generous cities in the United Kingdom to servicemen during the War. I must say that during my short time of a few weeks in their Technical College, I really enjoyed their almost free entertainment in the Music Hall, dance halls, and also the Theatre Royal, where the Doyly Carte Opera Company allowed us to see the whole of the Gilbert and Sullivan operas for 10 shillings, though up in the gods for that price! We were also allowed to travel on the trams free, for which we were issued with tokens.

With reference to the Gilbert and Sullivan operas, as a different opera was performed each weekday evening, I had to apply to the Commander in Charge of the Base for evening leave for at least two weeks. He was very interested in the programme which I showed him, and of which he was unaware. My request I am glad to say was granted, and he added that he also would be interested in this, and would be on the lookout for me when I was there. I was extremely lucky to be in the right place at the right time on that occasion, as that experience was I feel somewhat unique, like the operas themselves. In fact to this day I can recall these highly entertaining works very well, simply because having seen the whole range of them like this, almost as a study, you can appreciate the huge variation in the composition of the lyrics and music to address the subject matter. That few weeks in Glasgow I shall always remember as a significant time during my wartime service, and for which I am indeed thankful.

Early in 1945 I was drafted back to HMS *Victory* and thence to HMS *Collingwood* at Fareham, where I was to spend the rest of my time in the Royal Navy, though not I may say as I would have wished, since after the War I was offered a permanent Commission as an Electrical Officer, but my father would not let me take it up. When joining *Collingwood* I was given the rank of a Leading Radio Mechanic, which apart from better pay prospects, also led to other advantages as I became a Radar instructor there. So I got good weekend leave to go home, and was allowed a bicycle to move not only around the establishment but also the district, which proved to be a good advantage.

Of course the work that we were doing at *Collingwood* was very secret then, and at the same time very interesting. As a trained Gunner I was involved in the first Radar-controlled automatic gun, which was used in the Far East by the Americans to shoot down the Kamikaze suicide bombers. This British invention helped to end the War out there, by the defeat of the Japanese fleet. In fact we were working on this between VE-Day and VJ-Day later in the year.

One of the things I learnt at *Collingwood* was that the Wrens who had been taught separately in Radar mechanics were excellent at it. I suppose that as it was like scientific knitting it was easier for them to puzzle out. I can now well understand why they are an important part of a ship's crew, if only for this reason alone. I had never worked closely with women before, and so this was a new and enlightening experience. In later life as a result I realized the potential of the particular perception that women possess, and utilized this to good effect in business. Apart from this these very intelligent Wrens were most attractive, and were fun in our spare time. I had a happy time at *Collingwood* with frequent weekend leave, and after VE-Day my parents came down to the Grand Hotel at Southsea to stay so that I could visit them.

In the early part of 1946 I was offered a Permanent Commission in the Royal Navy as an Electrical Officer due to my exceptional training, which the Navy had invested in me. This required the agreement of my next of kin as it would involve electronics in submarines, as well as surface vessels. My father refused to agree to this, and added that I had had enough time enjoying myself in the Navy, and that it was now time to get down to doing a proper job! I need not comment further, except that this was a great disappointment to me, though I had at least justified my decision to run away from Eton College all those years ago. I admired the Navy still, and was sad to end my career in it. Mind you I was still destined to go to sea again in my own yachts, and to follow my Grandfather as the only other member of his family to be elected a member of the Royal Yacht Squadron, the most distinguished of Naval Clubs, and regarded as an Honour, particularly for an Able Seaman!

CHAPTER 9

My continuing life as a sailor, and some other highlights of ordinary life after the Royal Navy

ALL OF US HAD TO CONCERN ourselves after returning from World War Two with obtaining a living, and settling down to a more ordinary way of life, which to some of us, including myself, was not easy. I do not propose to bore the reader with the ordinary things of everyday life, as after my previous adventures that I have recorded, which hopefully have been of interest, reference to such daily matters I have endeavoured to avoid.

My father enabled me to have about six weeks rest before he arranged for my Articles of Apprenticeship as a solicitor to start. I have to explain that his firm in Birmingham was called Cottrell & Son, and had been going as solicitors from father to son for six generations since the Seventeenth Century. I was to be the seventh generation, which when I had qualified was acknowledged by Mr Lund, the then Secretary of the Law Society, as a record for the profession. I am glad to state that there was not to be an eighth generation, except by voluntary interest in the legal profession, which was in the event not to be expressed by any of my children. To be fair a form of succession in my young days was a carry forward of Victorian values, and hence my studies for a law degree at Cambridge, which was supported by both of my surviving grandparents on both sides of the family.

During my long leave my parents organized a two-week holiday in early June in Cornwall at Perranporth, in a house which they rented in conjunction with an aunt and uncle, along with two of my cousins. This I have always remembered, as the same eight of us had been on holiday together at Woolacombe on the outbreak of World War Two, and there we were to celebrate, and be united in our miraculous survival, as we had all survived close bombing attacks.

Of course after my Articles, I had to attend Law School, which in those days was run by the famous Gibson & Weldon. During this period late in 1949, my mother came up into my study one day, and said 'David, you are now 27, and it is time that you thought about getting married, as I want to have some grandchildren.' I replied that I was sorry but although I had presented quite a few nice girls to her to date, none of them had been quite as exceptional as my beloved Marylena, who I knew had got married during the War. To my astonishment about three weeks later my mother told me that her great friend, Olga St Aubrey Davies, who lived in our parish and knew Marylena well, had traced her to Great Comberton just around the Hill from us, and discovered that she had obtained a divorce, so that she was putting on a party for us to meet up again. This duly took place in January 1950, and there she was just as lovely as ever. I just could not believe my luck. So then followed a short courtship, lasting only a few weeks, before I popped the question. My proposal I am glad to say was accepted as her divorce had gone through, and we were married on 6 June 1950 on the hottest day in the year. The rest of my life really started from then, since Marylena has helped create it ever since, and is still lovely, and bossy, and interesting. We are both 81 now, and without her I am sure that I would not still be going strong. I have always been thankful that I waited for the right partner.

Thus I started work in my father's firm as a Partner in January 1951, since by now I had passed all the necessary exams. At that time I also agreed to help the late Douglas Barwell restore the Lower Avon Navigation, between Tewkesbury and Evesham, which with the collapse of the lock gates at Strensham, immediately upstream from Tewkesbury, seemed destined to be closed for ever. And so I was elected on to the Council of the Lower Avon Trust at their first meeting in January 1951. My service on that Council was to span the next 50 years, and so most of the rest of this memoir as we shall see emerges from my interest in the waterways. Certainly I would not wish to bore the reader with the ordinary progression of life in earning a living and bringing up a family.

The late Douglas Barwell was a brassfounder in Birmingham, and after the Inland Waterways Association was founded in 1946, by the late Robert Aickman, he was elected Hon Secretary of its

Midlands branch. He kept a motor cruiser on the River Severn at that time at Worcester. When on holiday he arrived at Strensham lock on the River Avon and found that he could not get through it because of the state of the upper gates. He then got in touch with the Navigation Company, which was virtually bust, and arranged to buy the company off them for £5000, which included the right to a rent charge of £400 in perpetuity payable by the Transport Commission (now British Waterways), and which is still paid annually. Douglas Barwell then ordered two new gates for the lock from the Commission. Our newly formed Council then assumed these obligations, and we were back in business, with the navigation usable as far as Pershore, where the millers still kept a barge to carry their wheat from Avonmouth. Above Pershore the navigation at that time was completely unusable, and it took us 14 more years to re-open it.

Little did I know at that time, taking part in this courageous enterprise which in fact was to be the forerunner nationally of many other such schemes, including railway restorations, that I was to end up leaving legal practice, and joining the boating industry. I was appointed by Barwell to the Operating Committee of the Trust, the first Chairman of which was Major General Sir Reginald Kerr, who at that time was Chairman of the Midlands Region of the British Transport Commission, which at the time controlled all forms of transport including road haulage. This was convenient to me as we held the Committee meetings in his offices in Birmingham.

As you would expect Sir Reginald was an excellent leader, and in no time we had the operational requirements of the navigation well looked after on the section which had been opened up. Of course Douglas Barwell had recruited me knowing that as a solicitor I could help deal with the Trust's legal side without incurring expense on advice where it could be avoided. The late Charles Beale of Birmingham was the Trust's official legal representative, he was a friend, and fellow member of our Club in Birmingham, so between us we saved them a lot of money as he was very generous to the trust when charging for his firm's work. In early 1954 Sir Reginald Kerr was appointed Chairman of the Inland Waterways Division of the British Transport Commission and departed to London. I was then appointed by Barwell in his place, with the direction that I was to try and tighten up on the law relating to the use of the river, as we were getting complaints about the use of speedboats. We had then to meet locally after that. We were naturally sorry to say goodbye to Sir Reginald, and I remember him saying to me that Barwell, whom he termed the Dictator, should be given unquestioning support, as he was clearly a first class leader, simply because he lived for the cause, and was always planning the next move. He said that whatever the rest of us might think we would not in his view succeed without his overpowering approach, which I am sure was correct. I am glad to say, as I was very busy at work and with a young family, that it was only a year later that I was transferred to a new Committee, as Chairman of the Byelaws Committee of the Trust, commissioned to draw up byelaws for regulating the navigation, as speedboat use was causing more problems, as by that time there were Sailing Clubs racing on the river. I had of course been advising the Operating Committee that legislation was necessary to control the misuse of the river, and to legalize our charging powers, which except for the Commercial use, relied on a tariff of donations only.

In the meanwhile my sailing life started, because my father-in-law Captain J.A.D.Perrins, who had been the owner of a six-metre yacht on the Hamble River before the War, and a member of the Household Brigade Yacht Club, got me a crewing job on a Shannon One Design, whilst out in Ireland on holiday at his house by Lough Derg. These were very fast 18ft-Gunter rigged boats specially designed by Morgan Giles Senior of Teignmouth for Lough Derg and the Dromineer Yacht Club. They also sailed Firefly dinghies there and I found that they were fun to sail in as well. When I got home on that first occasion, I bought my own Firefly dinghy to sail at the Avon Sailing Club, which was at that time based on the Avon at Twyning Fleet.

For the next three years we holidayed in Ireland with my father-in-law, until he unfortunately had to move away. So I attended several week-long August regattas there, and had the opportunity to crew in one of the Dun Laoghaire International Dragon Class one designs which was exciting, and great fun, plenty of laughter and Guinness in the pub nearby followed the racing.

I loved the time we had in Ireland, and I was glad some years later to be able to entertain some of those skippers, who like myself had taken to offshore sailing, on board my yacht at Cowes, when they were competing in the Admiral's Cup for Ireland. I had by 1956 joined the Royal Solent Yacht Club at Yarmouth Isle of Wight, and started sailing there in the Y class as a member of the crew. In the summer of 1957 I was staying at the George Hotel in Yarmouth, and was in the front hall having a drink, when the door opened and in came a priest, who came over to me immediately, and to my surprise greeted me as if a long lost friend. He was John Huggins, a boy in the Lower School when I left Eton College, and a member of the same house as me. He said he would never forget me as one of senior boys who terminated the bullying in the House at that time, which we had managed to deal with. I was very glad to know that I had at least done something useful whilst I was there. I cannot stand people who bully in what is thought a civilized society, it is totally unnecessary, and indeed evil.

In 1958 I bought my first offshore racing yacht, which was Fairey Atalanta designed by Uffa Fox and was numbered 61 in the class which was a one design. She would accommodate the whole family when we were on holiday, thereby saving us the expense of an hotel. I remembered that the finest looking ship in the Fleet at Scapa Flow was HMS *Dido*, and wanted that name, since Marylena had found that she was a goddess had a decent record. However the Admiralty had the right to that name, so we took up the Carthaginian name of that goddess, namely 'Elissa' which has been the registered name of all our yachts since then. I raced her for five seasons, and she won the first Round the Island race for the class, as well as another16 local prizes in her first year. She was a good boat, and with her self- draining cockpit very seaworthy.

Meanwhile after my father had retired, in 1959 I had gone into partnership with a good friend of mine William Kentish, whom I have already referred to as the Officer of the Watch on board HMS *Arethusa* in Scapa Flow during the War. His firm was James Kentish & Atkins, and on amalgamation we became Cottrell Son & Wm Kentish, and in 1962 built new offices in conjunction with several friends in other professions, as we could no longer house our expansion in our old Georgian office in Waterloo Street. (Bill

HMS Dido (Elissa) in the North Atlantic 1943

Kentish and I practised together for the next 10 years in complete harmony, never a cross word, until I decided to join the Marine Industry. It was a good move and we still keep in touch.) My mother had pre-deceased my father in 1957, and my father died in May 1960, and I am glad to record that all our differences that my time in the Royal Navy had caused had been long since forgotten, and that we had enjoyed a good relationship together as Partners, which had a lot to do with my dear wife. By that time I had become a director of several property companies, and in particular a small family Brewery with about 50 pubs around Birmingham and elsewhere. The three brothers who were running it were reaching retiring age, and they had only female heirs, so I advised them to sell up and enjoy life as the big groups were by then dominating the market. At the end they were so grateful for what I had done for them, they contributed to a new offshore racing yacht for me, so that made my job worthwhile! This would be *Elissa II*, and was a 31 ft Atalanta class yacht built by Fairey Marine at Hamble, and an Royal Ocean Racing Club handicap offshore racer.

I did less than a season's sailing in her, before she was rammed amidships on her mooring in the Hamble River by a steel boat out of control and holed. The insurance company paid up for repairing her, but would not agree to replace her, which I was advised to require as she would not again be suitable for racing, this was a great disappointment.

However by that time I also had a share in an X racing boat at Yarmouth, and in addition a friend whom I used to shoot with, Colonel Tony Somers, an Olympic yachtsman in the International Dragon Class, asked if I would like to come and crew in his Dragon. This was an opportunity that I jumped at due to my previous experience in racing in that class in Ireland.

Having no offshore seagoing vessel in 1964, and therefore missing the joys of being at sea, my wife and I considered the next move, as we had already sold our house in Yarmouth, rather foolishly, simply because our four children, or some of them, had got bored with the summer holiday there every year. So we commissioned the building at Beechman's yard at Tewkesbury of a 45-ton motor yacht with a funnel and two masts, so that we could house ourselves and several friends aboard. She was named *Elissa III*, registered at Gloucester, and designed by the late Leslie James of Weymouth, and carried a Scimitar Class 23ft-keel sailing boat aboard (these were designed by Laurent Giles and based on an X boat, though made of fibreglass). Also on board we carried a 20ft high-speed launch made by Windboats of Wroxham on the Broads. I managed to get a mud berth at Berthon's Yard at Lymington on the Solent for the summer season, and cruised her back to Tewkesbury for the winter, as she was a very good sea boat. She was launched in 1965, and taken to the Solent in the early part of 1966.

My Friend Tony Somers asked me if I could join him as his middle man in his Dragon for the Olympic Trial Regatta at Poole, run from the Royal Motor Yacht Club. This was a great invitation, and I suggested that I should take our motor yacht down as a Headquarters vessel. It was an exceptional occasion, to sail amongst our top class helmsmen, and to see at close quarters the difference between us ordinary helmsmen and them was an enlightening experience. I am glad to say that I was invited to the same event again in 1969, when rode to an anchor in Bournemouth Bay which saved us fighting the tide into and out of Poole Harbour. We managed to accommodate two Dragons and their crews aboard.

Otherwise we used the boat to cruise over to St Malo, the Channel Islands, Cherbourg, and Deauville with the family and friends, which was very nice. At this time Tony Somers had introduced me to the Royal Yacht Squadron, where I knew some of the members, and he had asked if he would allow him to put me up for membership. It was a great honour to be asked, let alone elected, and so I agreed to be put up, as if elected I would be the only member of my Grandfather's family to be so honoured. Once again I was lucky and was duly elected in 1970, an unusual honour for an Able Seaman of the Royal Navy. Some six years later our son Rupert was elected a member, also on the proposal of Tony Somers.

I must mention to the reader here perhaps the first incident of significant interest about my life after the Navy. Lord Runciman was the Commodore of the Squadron when I was elected, then he was succeeded by Major General the Earl of Cathcart. One day when I was talking to Tony Somers on the platform, Tony told the General that I found it difficult to understand why the Naval Members of the Squadron had to fly the Red Ensign, instead of the White Ensign of the Club. I then told the General that Vice Admiral Angus Cunninghame Graham had been my Captain on Russian Convoy and as a Naval Member could not fly the Naval Colours, whereas I who had been his Able Seaman messenger on board was flying the White Ensign on my yacht. I suggested to the General that perhaps the Army would not have allowed such a situation, and he agreed with me completely. He then saw to it that the rules were altered to rectify this, thus my title of an unusual Able Seaman was justified, and one up to the Army!

Having joined what was considered to be one of the most exclusive and premier Yacht Clubs, I felt that ownership of a motor yacht was no longer appropriate. Apart from this I wanted to get back into offshore racing for a while at least. So we sold the motor yacht, which ended up in French ownership in the Med, and we bought a new 41ft Dufour designed offshore sailing yacht built in La Rochelle. She was named by my daughter Sarah in the Hamble River *Elissa IV*, a lovely sloop, and very seaworthy. She was beautiful down below, with the lovely woodwork which the French are so good at, and my wife thought that she was the best of all our boats. I took her on the Cowes Dinard race every year, and we did some extensive cruising in her. Her end came in 1978 when my youngest son Mark got married and left sailing for a time as it was not his wife's scene. Whilst I had *Elissa IV* he had recruited the young crew necessary to do the forecastle work, it needed five to set and recover the Spinniker of 1000 square feet, so I realized that it was likely to be getting beyond us. We then bought our present boat which is a seventy foot narrow boat named *Elissa V*, on which we have since toured most of the Inland Waterway system that is navigable.

I must return now to the other things that I was, and to some extent am, involved in during everyday life until the present time. I have already referred to my decision with my wife's support to join the Marine Industry in 1969. Again this was a lucky one by chance, which arose from my involvement as Chairman of the

Byelaws Committee of the Lower Avon Navigation Trust. After several years of negotiation with the Ministry of Transport along with Charles Beale, our solicitor, and Mr Christie of Counsel, a waterways expert, we had failed to convince the Ministry that we were entitled to have byelaws. Then suddenly some fool with an overloaded boat called the *Darlwynne* overturned it in the Barmouth Estuary with a grave loss of life. The usual enquiry followed, and it was found to be necessary that in future all navigation authorities should have regulating byelaws. Then unbelievably the Ministry wrote to us and wanted to know what we were doing about making byelaws! They then stated that they should be re-submitted and would in the circumstances be passed. What a way to run a country!

The outcome of all of this was that Douglas Barwell thanked me, and my Committee, for all that we had done. He later on said to me that unfortunately we had caused the Trust an incidental problem, because although we had stopped the misuse of the navigation, and we had legalized the charging powers and the recovery of tolls, we had because of the licensing by law dried up the previous donation income. The number of moorings on the navigation would be insufficient to balance the Trust's budget, and he estimated that we would need an extra 100 moorings on the river to make good the deficit. He asked me therefore what I would do, as my next task, to make this good! I accepted the challenge, and said that as I was at the time a director of a development and building company in Birmingham, I would see if they would consider building a marina, and if so I would approach Beechams of Tewkesbury to see if they would jointly build a marina with us on the unused land next to their Boatyard. This I did and I was authorized to open negotiations with Jim Beecham, whose Company had built our motor yacht, and with whom I had served on the Trust's Council for 18 years. He and his directors agreed to give us a long lease of the proposed marina land, but they did not want to be involved financially, although they would give us every help possible in respect of planning. Our directors agreed to go ahead on this basis. So I asked Jim Beecham if he would arrange a meeting with the Borough Surveyor to discuss the matter from the planning point of view to see if such a scheme might be acceptable to Tewkesbury. He said that he would arrange this and be in touch with me.

As I had heard nothing from Jim Beecham after waiting three weeks, I called in at his office and was met by his son Paul, who stated that his father had been taken very ill and was at the moment in the Frenchay Hospital in Bristol. So I asked that when he was well enough would he tell him to get in touch, and also asked him to give him my best wishes for a speedy recovery. A few days later a deliveryman saw through the window of the Beechams' house a body, and when the police got in they discovered four bodies: of Paul's parents and his grandparents. Of course Paul Beecham was arrested and tried, and sent to Broadmoor. I had thought that that was the end of that matter as far as I was concerned. It was a great shock as I had grown to know and like that family during the many months that their firm were building our yacht.

I had after that considered that my approach to Beecham Marine would be finished in view of what had happened. However a few weeks later in 1969, I needed a pot of varnish to take down to my boat, and as the yard was still open, I went in and saw Bill Holyoake, the master boatbuilder and a surviving director of the Company, who sold me the varnish. He asked me, as he had got on with me very well whilst building our yacht, whether I would continue negotiations for building a marina, but as Paul Beecham had embezzled most of the Company's funds, we would have to purchase the yard as well as leasing the marina land. He then gave me details of the creditors' meeting in May that year, and told me that the boat owners on the site would also be bidding for the company. To cut a long story short we ended up with a situation where the directors of the development company I had helped to create withdrew from the matter, though one of them, a good friend of mine at Arden House School, Richard Harris, supported me, and is a Shareholder to this day in the Tewkesbury Marina, and my wife and I decided to buy the yard and marina site on the basis of the report by my development company Auditors. We succeeded in our bid and I was glad to offer the surviving directors, Denys Shirlaw the Chairman whom I took over from, and Bill Holyoake, a continuation of their shareholdings as well as continuing as directors.

So then I went with Bill Holyoake, who had consulted with Walcon Marine over a draft plan for a marina basin to accommodate 125 boats, to see Mr Broxton, the Tewkesbury Borough Surveyor. He said that he was sure that his planning committee would approve our plan as it would be excellent for the town, and if we wished to enlarge the marina in future, we should indicate where we wanted to expand it. If we then let him have the revised plan he could get it approved within three weeks. The planning permission duly arrived two weeks later, and at no cost to the company, what a difference from the expense and overbearing bureaucracy of today! Meanwhile we had set up a separate development company to build the marina in October 1969, and we immediately recruited the necessary construction team and started digging. At the 1970 Boat Show in London which my wife, who was the Company Secretary, and I attended, we met Rear Admiral Percy Gick, a great character, who was then President of the National Yacht Harbour Association (The Chairman and Chief Executive), and signed up for that important organization, which enabled us to gain a lot of information with reference to matters like berthing conditions.

The next two years were spent in digging the first marina basin with our own equipment and tipper lorries to dispose of the soil, while running the boatyard company as well. Apart from being a master boatbuilder, building almost exclusively seagoing yachts, Bill Holyoake had been trained as an apprentice at Bathhursts yard in Tewkesbury when they were building motor torpedo boats during the War, was also an excellent engineer and supervised everything we did over the next 30 years until his retirement. Early in 1972 we opened our first basin for 125 berths, practically all of which were full by the end of the year, and Douglas Barwell was well pleased, and admitted to me that he thought it a bit of a gamble!

By 1970 I found that I had my hands too full to go on in daily practice in the law, since by then I had trained as a yacht broker and as a salesman for the new boats under construction, and was earning a salary as the Chairman and Managing Director of both Companies, so I transferred to being a consultant solicitor only. As I had always wanted to be involved in the creative side of things, which the law does not directly involve, I was glad about this change of career which I undertook with my family's agreement. We went on to develop a 350-berth Marina, which served both the River Severn level as well as the River Avon in the end, and was to be one of the largest inland marinas in the country, and we developed some good houses surrounding part of it. Our younger son Mark took over from me as Managing Director in 1991, and although I continued as Chairman until 2002, when all of us original directors except for my wife retired, I still have an interest as a Shareholder. It proved for me to be a worthwhile creative effort.

The reader may wonder why I have gone into so much detail about this marina building, the reason being to give a backdrop to the following chapter about my time on the Councils of the leisure marine industry, which may be of more interest.

CHAPTER 10

My time of service on the councils of the British Boating Industry, and other bodies

WHEN I JOINED BEECHAM MARINE LTD, which continued to build boats until the Government in 1975 wrecked the boat building side of the industry by charging 25% VAT on boats for a year, when it was 8% on everything else, as I have related already I became a yacht broker, and then joined the Association of Brokers and Yacht Agents. So in 1970 I attended their AGM for the first time, and as they were short of people on the committee I accepted nomination and was elected. I was then to serve on their committee and joint committee and that of the Yacht Brokers, Designers and Surveyors Association, of which I was also a member, until 1994 when they made me an Honorary Fellow of the Association. With my legal training I had been able to not only help them revise all their contracts, to enable them stand up in court, but also to draw up the documents required to eventually amalgamate the two then existing Broker's Associations at no cost.

In 1972 Admiral Gick invited me to join the Council of the then National Yacht Harbour Association (now known as The Yacht Harbour Association), he had got to know me by then, as he came on one occasion to view our new marina. I think that he also had in mind the advantage of having legal knowledge at hand without the usual costs! This was to prove one of the most interesting periods of my life as I was to end up being elected Vice President, then President, and finally Vice Chairman (Inland), covering many years up to January 1991. Likewise along with my solicitor friend the late Norman Smith, who owned Salterns Marina at Poole in Dorset, I was able to help in drawing up and revising the legal documents used in the Marina Industry.

I was eventually elected to serve on the Ship & Boatbuilders Federation (now the British Marine Federation), and served for

YACHT BROKERS, DESIGNERS & SURVEYORS ASSOCIATION

This is to certify that Council have elected

David V. S. Cottrell

HONORARY FELLOW BROKER MEMBER

David, this is to simply record our grateful thanks for the significant contribution you have made to the Association.

In particular your work in connection with the Brokers code, agreements and the merger of the Associations, is appreciated and to the benefit of all members. Thank you for your untiring and continuing assistance.

President _____

(Tony Staton-Bevan)

Chief Executive _____

(Rae Boxall)

Date 13th November, 1995

Author's Certificate of Honorary Membership of Yacht Brokers, Designers and Surveyors Association

about 18 years, ending as Chairman of the Midland Boatbuilders Association. So that I can record that I had an interesting and active life in the yachting industry during those years. In addition I served for seven years during the seventies and early eighties on the Royal Yachting Association Cruising Committee in London representing the industry. The only significant contribution that I can remember making via the RYA was as an offshore sailor to get the Committee to ask Trinity House to either remove all unlit buoys around the coast of the UK or light them at night, since with solar technology this was now reasonable. Hitting one of their unlit buoys could cause a great deal of damage to a yacht, and there were quite a number of them, including the Admiralty buoys in the Solent, which were eventually removed, and other navigation marks. The Chairman of the Committee at that time was Captain McMullen RN(Retd), who needless to say always got on with me very well, as we ex-Naval men seem to do, and he was most supportive of my cause in this respect. We were entirely successful in achieving this objective in the end I am glad to say.

In 1979, by which time I had been elected during the preceding year as President of the National Yacht Harbour Association (Executive Chairman and Chief Executive) in succession to Brian Folley, one of the Founders of Harleyford, I was asked to attend an International Conference in Cairo along with our Vice President the late Colin Perkin of Ramsgate Harbour Marina, and a Professor of Oceanography from York University, whose name I am unable to recall.

We were asked by Mrs Thatcher's Government to undertake the task of advising the Egyptian Government on creating tourist facility boats on the Nile, the Suez Canal, Aboukir Bay, and in Alexandria Eastern Harbour. The Professor was to advise on tourist facilities in relation to the Red Sea area, where diving to view the amazing coral reefs had become very popular. Our Embassy out there was to be available to help us if required.

The three of us British Government Delegates were briefed in London, by Mr Eleithy of the Egyptian Embassy, and we were flown out to Cairo subsequently at the Egyptian Government's expense. We were given some clear details of what was expected, and so we took out a lot of information supplied by our Industry, who gave us a lot of very good information based on the brief. The cost of the Mission was entirely paid for by the Egyptian Government. Every Government in Europe was given a similar briefing along with the United States of America, which was asked to send two delegations, one from each coast.

In early 1980 we arrived in Cairo to be put up in Shepherd's Hotel, along with the delegates from all the other countries, for a period of two weeks. Whilst we used to generally have drinks with the Americans before dinner in the evening, which was rather natural, we also arranged each night to have dinner with a different delegation. On the last day of the visit a conference was held at which each delegation had to speak to a paper, declaring their recommendations to the Egyptian Government. Quite an undertaking for us in the end!

As an extra we were flown to Luxor, to advise on the facilities for tourism there, and to visit the tombs of the Kings and Queens, which was an amazing event, something unique which I would recommend to anyone. We had already been shown around the Pyramids and the Cairo Museum whilst in Cairo, so we could understand something of the history of what we saw there. We were put up in the new air-conditioned wing of the famous Winter Palace Hotel in Luxor, built by the British. And I remember going with Colin Perkin for a sail on the Nile in a felucca. We sailed across the great river, which must be about a mile wide there, and on the opposite bank upsteam were a lot of naked women doing their dobying (clothes washing), whereupon our skipper sailed into the middle of them, and proceeded to have an argument with one whom he said was his girlfriend. Whilst she was interesting to view, the encounter was a bit embarrassing, to say the least, but we had a good laugh afterwards. We were taken back to Luxor on the starboard tack, and as we approached the mooring by the hotel, the skipper indicated to me that he wished me to take the helm; as I said to Colin afterwards he knew who was the experienced helmsman! And with that he climbed to the top of the mast, and those ones are quite high, like a monkey, and furled the sail most beautifully like an umbrella.

We were taken to Port Said in an excellent Mercedes air-conditioned bus, and when we got there outside the Governor's

Palace, a call went out for the British Delegation to step down, and we were then shown into the Palace front door whilst the bus went on. There we were introduced to the Governor and his guests, and the Governor, who said to me that we were the most favoured country in Egypt, because of what we had done for them when we were in charge there after the two wars, asked me if I would stand next to him whilst he took the salute at a march past by a guard and band of the Egyptian Army, playing incidentally Colonel Bogey. In the circumstances this was a great honour, because all the other delegations were seated at the other side of the parade ground. There was the usual reception afterwards for all of us, and we were then taken by boat to Port Fouad on the other side of the harbour at the entrance to the Suez Canal, to consider a projected marina development there. I knew that when we got back to Shepherd's in Cairo that evening, we might well be asked over drinks by our American friends why I was invited to stand by the Governor that morning to take the salute. I was able to assure them that the American notion that we ruled always as colonialists was demonstrably incorrect, and that we ruled for a time in Egypt so as to try and help them stabilize the country after the Turks withdrew following the First World War, and they had always been grateful for what we had done for them. Of course they said what about the Suez conflict? Fortunately I could answer this as the Egyptian authorities had already briefed us that they regarded this as an unfortunate misunderstanding on both sides. At Port Fouad we viewed the moorings at the Yacht Club, for yachts going or coming through the Canal, which were unsatisfactory. The main reason being that the bilge discharges from the big ships using the Canal caused a certain amount of fuel oil to drift into the little harbour there, and then this fouled up the topsides of the yachts, which was obvious to all of us. The Chief Engineer of the Suez Canal Company was introduced to me after he had given his presentation to all of us. I had taken out with me some copies of a book that we had produced as a result of an International Seminar just before then at Southampton University, and I suggested to him that with his expertise he could build this small marina himself from information in the book. Indeed there was a description of a floating automatic oil boom in the book to be put in the marina

entrance to solve that problem, and we would put him in touch
with the suppliers.

The next day we were taken to Ismalia halfway down the Suez
Canal where we where given a banquet by the Canal Company at
their headquarters, and taken for a trip on the canal. We were
shown the site of a marina near the headquarters, and were
expected to advise on how to develop it. The following day we
were taken to stay the night in a hotel which had been the Royal
family's palace in Alexandria, a lovely place on the Mediterranean
coast. The Egyptian Tourist Minister had previously invited the
British Delegation to a private dinner in his house in Alexandria,
which very much underlined their good relations with Britain.
This is interesting because President Mubarak had just started his
Presidency at that time, and we felt this to be an unexpected
privilege for us. The next day we were taken to the magnificent
Roman Eastern Harbour at Alexandria, where we were given
lunch in the Alexandria Yacht Club. We were asked to plan a
marina for at least 500 yachts there, and provide the necessary
breakwater to attenuate the swell, which the occasional easterly
wind caused there. We then returned across the desert road to
Cairo where two days later each delegation had to make their
presentation to the Egyptian Tourist Minister. We then flew home
by Egyptian Airways, but got diverted to Paris, because due to
heavy snow the runways at Heathrow were closed. We were put
up in a very nice Hotel in Paris for the whole of one day but could
not go out as we were on call to resume our journey. The next
day I got in touch with our Embassy who arranged for us as we
were on government business to fly to Heathrow by special
arrangement with Air France. So ended a very memorable
experience to which there was to be a sequel.

Mr Eleithy of the Egyptian Embassy in London had accompanied us outwards to Egypt and briefed us throughout the trip out
there. Two years later, several of the firms that we had put forward
as having answered our appeal for contractors before we left the
UK had been awarded contracts out there. Notably British firms
landed the contracts for marinas in Aboukir Bay and most
important the marina at Ismalia. The Americans got the development at Alexandria. Mr Eleithy got in touch again with the NYHA

The Author giving the UK presentation to the Egyptian Ministry of Tourism

and arranged that we should be flown out as guests of the Egyptian Government, to go and view the effects of the contracts awarded to British firms, and comment on the results to the officials in their tourist Ministry.

This was a very interesting follow up mission, and I glad to say that the work carried out was well thought of. Amongst other things we were given lunch again at the Suez Canal headquarters, and inspected the new marina at Ismalia which was a success and filling up with yachts. After lunch we were taken on a trip up the canal, in their inspection vessel, and what was amazing was that in the two years since we had last seen it they had finished digging the double canal, which now enabled ships to proceed up the canal without a convoy system, as it was now a form of dual carriageway type of waterway. When we were there previously the super-tankers were proceeding through in convoy, and they were only two thirds laden. They were proceeded by a 90,000-ton tanker, which when it got to Port Said topped up the supertanker, which could then proceed into the Mediterranean fully laden. There two years later we found the supertankers proceeding fully laden, without the need to be in convoy, and the consequent costs that that involved, and also the costs of having to stop in order to top up. The dredging had been carried out by a German firm with the largest dredger that you ever saw. We also were taken to Port Fauod to view the small marina that the canal engineers had built according to the advice in the NYHA book that I had given them two years before. It was, as I thought it would be, a complete success, and the floating oil boom from the UK was working well.

Next we were flown to Luxor to see what had happened there. In the taxi coming from the airport the driver asked Colin and me whether we were both British, and when we said that we were he said that we were very welcome in Luxor. He went on to say that Luxor was built by the British, and that they built the railway and freshwater canal and that everything still worked, unlike the efforts of other countries later involved, and so the people of Luxor we always be grateful for what the British had done for them. This accolade we both felt came from the heart, and was worth recording. We had recommended that the broken pavements leading along the waterfront and also to the Karnak Temple should be repaired, and a street washing system introduced. The Egyptians had run a horse and trap taxi service to the temple when we were first there, and the tourists liked this. But inevitably the horse dung built up, and caused a problem for the pedestrians. I had told them that when I was young this trouble was overcome by using crude water hydrants to wash the streets down early in the day. I always remember this happening in Oxford Street for example. Accordingly I found that all the pavements had been repaired, some Sykes Diesel Pumps had been installed to pump up the Nile, and the streets were clean.

They then took us to Aboukir Bay on the Mediterranean Coast where Nelson won his famous victory of the Battle of the Nile. It was a lovely spot where the National Nautical College is situated and where a new British built marina is now situated. It was interesting to note that the area around the main road leading to Alexandria was being cultivated in the Nile Delta area where when we travelled through it previously there had only been desert. Our Guides told us that the Government had to find food for a population of people expanding at the rate of a million *per annum*, to a large extent due to asylum seekers coming across the desert, mostly from the war-torn Sudan, and also from Libya, so this expansion of food production was a priority. The Egyptians had been helped in the process of dealing with this problem by the Americans, who had showed them how to reclaim the desert. The process was to dig a trench around about a square mile of desert, pipe the silt water of the Nile delta into the trench and then plant a row of Eucalyptus trees in the trench. These would grow very quickly due to the fertility of the desert sand and the Nile water, and they would form the very necessary windbreak for crops, which could then be planted within months. I forgot to mention that when passing through the Delta area we stopped to look at the more ancient civilization methods. We saw there in real life a donkey at work propelling a lifting wheel over a well to irrigate the crops, with a small lad holding a carrot in his hand, and a stick in the other. Well then I knew where that expression came from! What a lovely scene!

Perhaps I have dwelt too long on these wonderful visits to Egypt, but it such an interesting place. The Suez Canal, the Pyramids, the Valley of the Kings and the nearby Mausoleum of Queen Hatchetsut, (the only female Pharoah, who had to dress as a man!), the Karnak Temple, the Roman city and harbour of Alexandria, and not least the great city of Cairo and the Nile, are all very unique and wonderful to have visited.

There were one or two highlights in my term as either Vice President or President of NYHA which are worth recording before closing. Firstly when I was Vice President during Brian Folley's term of office, which in those days was three years under the rules, he had a relative who was Captain of HMS *Repulse*, a nuclear submarine in Faslane, Scotland. Brian arranged a visit to the ship in conjunction with a visit to some of the Scottish marinas. We flew to Glasgow and went by coach to Edinburgh were we were to stay for several nights, and we inspected the site of a proposed marina by the Forth Bridge. Then we went the next day over to Faslane to have lunch in the Wardroom aboard the submarine. I remember going into the huge missile compartment and also the torpedo room forward. What a vast ship she was compared with the submarines that I had known, it was like being in an underwater Cruiser, as in fact it was of about the same tonnage of a Cruiser. As usual the Navy gave us a very good party in the Wardroom, which was luxurious compared with what one expected of a submarine. Next day we completed our tour of several west coast marinas and flew back to London.

During my term of office as President we produced the first code of practice for marinas, and also we instituted an assessment of marina facilities in the form of a gold anchor award scheme so to indicate to customers, rather like the hotel industry, what the customer could expect to find when booking into a marina. This has been found ever since then to be very useful to the boating public.

The Council of the Association as I have already described kept me quite busy during my three years as Chairman and Chief Executive. Apart from what you have already read, I had to deal with two summer visits abroad to both Holland and the Brittany marinas. The visit to Holland, where boating, unlike in Britain, is a way of life, was very interesting indeed. I remember going to one marina on the coast where we had lunch in the brand new Yacht Club, and the marina had just been opened a month or two before, exclusively for Ocean racing yachts, and it was practically full. Our hosts asked to be forgiven as the turf outside the clubhouse had not been completed! I asked how long they had taken to build this marina for 500 yachts, and they said one year only from start to finish. This period included the planning procedure. I told them that such a thing would be impossible in Britain, because of our ever increasing bureaucracy, which as I write is even worse now.

Our visit to France was equally interesting as we went from Portsmouth to St Malo and picked up a coach to go and stay in a good Hotel in Dinan as our base to start with. We went down to La Rochelle and the largest marina in Europe. Then we went on to La Boule marina, which is one quarter of a mile offshore over a bridge to a lagoon, for 500 yachts. This somewhat unique marina is in the Bay of Biscay and the vast lagoon is man-made of granite boulders, with a club, hotels, restaurants, and shops, all offshore, vaguely like Brighton marina. A new concept in marina building which I thought would be exactly right for West Bay near Bridport in Dorset, where a refuge harbour was badly needed. Next we went on to Brest which is another of the great French marinas, and which dwarf any similar developments in the UK.

The Mayor of Brest spoke the most excellent English, and welcomed us to a banquet. He told me that what the French really would like the British to do was to build a marina on the North Cornish Coast so that their very large seagoing yachts could put in on their way to Scotland after crossing the channel. Otherwise if they went into Falmouth on the way, it took nearly an extra day wasting time, due to the tide changing whilst going round Lands End, as I knew only too well. The other marinas, on our way back to St Malo, were also visited by our coach party of UK Marina operators. We had enjoyed a very informative visit for which were very grateful to the French industry.

After we got back the Managing Director of Rank Marine International Ltd, the late Captain J.A. Hans Hamilton RN (retd) made a report on the visit, making clear that the French have an altogether different attitude to providing leisure facilities for their population than the British. In his view the British were consumed with jealousy about other people's leisure pursuits, (nothing has changed since then, for instance, and though I have never been a hunting man, look at the recent legislation to stop the control of foxes, shooting them with the near certainty of wounding a lot of them rather than hunting them), and would do everything they could to stop other pursuits happening in which they do not have an interest.

I will quote Captain Hans Hamilton's exact words

The inland water areas give access to usage by the less well off, and much trouble is taken to provide cheap unguarded moorings for young families. Altogether the French have clearly approached the boating leisure industry in a different spirit and philosophy, resulting in support from their inhabitants, rather than the jealous snipery and cliquiness inherent in Britain.

This statement I regard as most important not only for the marina industry in England, but also elsewhere in this land. I believe that at any rate the Scots are more generously minded towards their people. I shall be 82 years old during this year, and the only task that I have left is as Chairman of a brand new Charitable Trust, just formed six months ago. It is named The Stratford & Warwick Waterways Trust, and was formed in October 2004, and has just qualified for registration under the Charities Act. Exactly the same type of people that I have already related opposed the opening of the Lower Avon Navigation 50 years ago are doing the same now, in opposing the further extension of the same river as far as Warwick. And as I am one of the last of the original members of the LANT Council who overcame that opposition, I have been elected to be their Chairman in order to defeat the 'jealous snipery and cliquiness' of the people of a minority, I am sure, because I am the only member of the Executive Committee at present not of that County, of the people of Warwickshire. Any reader who wishes to support me in this cause can log on to www.swwaterway.co.uk., and they will be doing the country as a whole, and its tourist interests, a great service as the Warwickshire County Council is at present our main opposition, and we are determined to defeat them in the same way that I and my colleagues did under the late Douglas Barwell over 50 years ago.

When we got back from France and reported to our Council, a number of important decisions were made. Through the good offices of my successor as President the late Norman Smith of Poole Harbour Yacht Club Marina (now known as Salterns Marina, and run by his son) and the Planning Officer at Poole, and following a meeting with the Environment Minister responsible, the late Sir Giles Shaw MP and his civil servant, we arranged at their suggestion to put on a national conference at Poole to determine future planning policy. In the event we took over in the autumn of 1982 the Sandbanks Hotel at Poole for this great meeting, which comprised, apart from the DOE civil servants, about 100 planning officers from all over the country, but likewise the same number of marina operators. This was a huge success. A new planning PPG document came out of it advising Local Authorities that in view of the national shortage of marinas they were not to oppose the development of them in suitable locations unless for technical reasons. The result of this was a rash of suitable, and indeed epic marinas in most places were they were needed. These included, for example, most of the marinas in Wales, including Swansea and Cardiff, and several more, also in Scotland, but most important, England, where we got through several in the Southampton area, such as Ocean Village, Hythe, and Port Solent at Portsmouth. Obviously the anti-British people in Brussels have managed to overturn this, as this planning policy no longer exists, so I am informed. At the present time I have been informed through an article in the TYHA magazine that we are now facing, according to British Waterways, a completely similar position on the Inland Waterways. Why, we may well ask? Well it is for the same reason that I have described above, and which fits in with the description given by the late Captain Hamilton.

I retired from office immediately following that successful Conference at Poole, though later on became Vice Chairman (Inland) under a constitutional re-organization until I retired in 1991. However just before the Poole Conference, the late Colin Perkin and I arranged to go and see the then Minister in charge of marinas at the DOE, who was by then Lord Strathclyde, specifically about two prospective marinas in Dorset and Cornwall. These were vital to the county's interests, and were being blocked as usual by the respective County Councils. Probably few of my readers will be aware that Lyme Bay between Weymouth and Salcombe in Devon is a long way across, and needs a refuge marina about halfway. We had laid down in our planning advice for marinas that 30 nautical miles was the maximum distance to allow for between marinas, and only Dorset and Cornwall exceeded this on the South Coast.

The Minister and his civil servant, I wish that I could remember his name, because he gave me some important help in another matter, could not in the end help us. It was too good to expect that the political situation in those two counties would be overcome by the nation's interests as might be expressed by the government of the day. The French Ministry for Marinas – mind you, they think that marinas are important in France, unlike the English in their country – had been kind enough to obtain for me a copy of the full plans for La Boule Marina. As I have previously mentioned we were very taken with that marina in the Bay of Biscay, and I had felt that it would be just right for a site in the middle of Lyme Bay where a refuge marina is badly needed.

So we danced this substantial portfolio of plans in front of the Minister, and said – there you are this will fit most beautifully at West Bay near Bridport in Dorset, give local employment which we know is very badly needed, and due to its design in a lagoon one quarter of a mile off the beach, it will not affect the existing uses either of the beach, or the existing harbour and its fishing boats. It should only cost the Government the same as the French, about £55 million, or less, as the granite for the breakwaters is nearer at hand. To put it mildly they were perplexed, and immediately said that any such scheme would have to be paid for by our industry.

We told them that our industry did not have the capability to carry out the private Act of Parliament that would be required, or the 40 year finance that French marinas had access to through their Government, who owned most French marinas, and leased them back to the industry or local communities to operate. We stated that quite apart from this no marina operator would be prepared to put a Private Bill through Parliament with all the costs involved, knowing how the jealous snipery and cliquiness of the landowners and some of the people involved with the Dorsetshire County Council would react without Government pressure. Of course our request was immediately refused within a matter of days. I always have wondered what happened to that beautifully bound volume of plans we handed over, it was too big for their shredder!

We also put before them a plan for a refuge marina in Hayle Bay near St Ives on the north coast of Cornwall, which I have already referred to, and which the Mayor of Brest had said the French very much needed, and not least ourselves. We told the Minister that this was a much smaller scheme costing only about £7 million, and handed over a plan that Mr Peter De Savery had produced, and which his development company was prepared to carry out. However Mr De Savery had made it quite clear to us that he was not prepared to go ahead with this plan, which would have great economic benefits for that area of Cornwell, unless the Government gave its backing. He, rightly in our view, required the Government to put a Bill through Parliament to authorize the scheme, so as to avoid the extra cost of a public enquiry estimated at least £1 million, which he was not prepared to fund to enable the usual English landowner objections, and indeed the jealous snipery and cliquiness of some of the English people of that area. Lord Strathclyde, the Minister, asked why the French could not use Falmouth, and as I have already related, I said that they would be on their way to Scotland and did not have the time to waste in getting round Lands End. He said that they had a long way to go to Scotland, they must have big boats, and why did they particularly want to visit Scotland? I was glad to assure him that the French had not only the largest marina in Europe, at La Rochelle, but they also had some of the largest yachts, and their affinity with Scotland was of course a matter of history. The Minister turned this request down flat as I suspect some of his fellow Cornish Peers in the House of Lords had already briefed him on the attitude of the County Council down there.

Anyway that had concluded our agenda, and the Minister had to leave in a hurry to go to the House. We were for a minute or two left with his civil servant, and I asked if I could raise a matter with him, which was unconnected with the business on the agenda, and in connection with the Inland Waterways. He agreed, and so I asked if he could help me as President of the Gloucester & Hereford Branch of the Inland Waterways Association over the imminent proposal of the Gloucestershire County Council to fill in and forever block the Stroudwater & Thames and Severn Canal at Stroud in order to construct the new proposed by-pass at Stroud. I told him that there was an active Canal Restoration Society there, of which I was a member, and indeed I had given them a dragline to help them with their work. The Canal Society had tried to get agreement with the County Council to allow for a diversion of the Canal round and under the by-pass route, so that the eventual restoration of the canal would be possible. I therefore asked if someone from his Ministry could as soon as possible meet the Gloucestershire County Highways Committee representatives in Stroud to inspect the proposal before it was too late. I explained that the canalside walk in this valley was such an important amenity for the residents, and this could be easily understood if the journey was made by train from Paddington, as from the stop at Kemble the route of the Canal was very visible as the train proceeded down the valley.

The Minister's civil servant said he would look into it. To my surprise he rang me up three weeks later, and stated that he had been down to inspect this canal, and had met the Highways Committee of the County Council at Stroud, and that they had accepted the Minister's requirement that they should make provision for the future restoration of the canal. He told me that he fully agreed with my observation about the importance of the canal as an amenity in that valley. As the reader can imagine I was highly delighted that at least our visit had achieved something of value. In fact this matter had in turn drawn the attention of the County Council to the importance of the waterways in their area, and I am glad to say that since then they have given full and very valuable support to the Canal Society, as well as to the waterways elsewhere in their County. I am hopeful that my new Restoration Trust project in Warwickshire will by persuasion likewise enable them to withdraw their present support for the jealous snipers and cliques of their county.

I mentioned earlier that in 1982 I was the President of the Gloucestershire & Herefordshire Branch of the Inland Waterways Association. I had in fact joined the Association in the 1950s soon after meeting its Founder the Late Robert Aickman, who was serving on the Lower Avon Navigation Trust's Council from the time that I joined it in 1951. He was a great man, very erudite, I suppose from being an author, and made wonderful speeches, always choosing the right words, and never being too long winded. We became good friends, and indeed I managed to get him appointed as a Consultant to the National Yacht Harbour Association on the subject of inland waterways, until the time of his death, and he gave us a lot of good advice. I was therefore an active member of the Association when they decided to form local county branches. I was therefore invited to join the first Committee in 1972, and have served as a member of it ever since, except for the years 1976-7 when I was serving as High Sheriff of the Counties of Hereford & Worcester. I had been advised during my year in office in that capacity to cease to serve on all public bodies so as to maintain, quite rightly, the independence of the Crown. When I returned to the fold in 1977, the Branch elected me as their first and only President to date, which is an honour, though it does carry responsibility, as I have had to assume the Chairman-ship of the Branch on two occasions when other people have not been available.

On the first occasion that the Branch failed, in about the year 1975, the then Hon Secretary Reg Beagley and I held a special general meeting to try and recruit a new Committee, as the previous one had resigned as a whole over a dispute. This concerned the then Stroudwater Canal Society and those running the Branch. I never quite understood it, but our new Committee was formed on the basis that we would make peace, which we duly did. I mention this as the new members who joined us on the Committee after that did sterling work. Amongst them were Gordon Lowthian, our Hon Treasurer, and who still supports me on the new Avon Trust, and Des Pinnock who became our Hon Secretary, and now is the very successful Membership Secretary of the Cotswold Canals Trust (which now includes the previous Stroudwater Canal Trust). Most noteworthy of all, we recruited Graham Ettles, who has been ever since our long serving Committee member, and to whom I wish to pay special tribute, as he has served as Chairman twice, as well as Hon Secretary and Treasurer. He has also ensured over many years that we had endless fund raising talks and events, in order to raise funds for the two Canal Trusts in our area.

The Inland Waterways Association has been of immense importance in ensuring that the River navigations in the area are preserved. Sadly we failed to overcome the landowner opposition to the rebuilding of the River Wye Navigation as far as Hereford, even though we had the support of the Hereford City Council and the Proprietors of the Wye Navigation. Again the unpleasant attitude of the upper class English people, so well described by Captain Hamilton, prevailed to stop the majority of our population being able to enjoy the surroundings of this famous river. Even so I, as long as I shall live, and my friends, will continue to fight against these selfish people and in the end I am sure that we shall win through. We have some influential people on our side. Prince Charles is the Patron of the Cotswold Canals Trust, and Timothy West is the Patron of the Stratford and Warwick Waterways Trust. We only need one for the River Wye! The other waterway that our IWA branch has always supported is the Hereford and Gloucester Canal Society and this is making lively progress, simply because it is supported by all the Local Authorities for once, and surprisingly by the landowners, who are exceptionally decent English people.

I have now covered the whole extent of my experience relating to nautical matters, which is the intention of this book, and I do not wish to bore the reader with the progress of normal family life, or that of earning a living, with which we are all faced. But what I may have achieved at all in public life is due to having a happy and stable background, and I must forever be grateful to my dear wife and our two sons and two daughters and their families for all the support they have given me in this respect. My wife has throughout the years been tireless at the same time in raising money for other charities in the area, and still serves on the Gloucestershire Historic Churches Trust, and she is still beautiful at the age of 81 and going strong.

There are however two aspects of my experience in life, which are in no way nautical, or have any connection with the intention of these memoirs, nor do they have any humorous content. I have recorded my legal career briefly, and the advantages it gave me in serving commerce and industry. The Law is without doubt the cement of civilized society, and thankfully the vast majority of the population understand this. The only thing that bothers me about it is that one branch of it, namely the English Common Law, lets neighbours down continuously, and causes endless problems that nobody seems to want to solve. Some people will probably not want to be involved in reading my comments on this.

The other aspect which might be of interest is the function of a High Sheriff, which not many people may be aware of. When I fulfilled this function I kept a diary, and therefore my record is in that form. So these two forms of memoir I have felt it would be better to deal with in the manner of appendices hereafter, as a conclusion to this account for those readers who may be interested.

Appendix I

The diary of The High Sheriff of Hereford and Worcester 1976/7

This appendix is included in these memoirs merely as a matter of interest to those who have no idea of the kind of functions performed by High Sheriffs some of which date back for over 1000 years. Some readers will be content to see a summary of this long winded diary which is as follows:

High Sheriff's Engagements

1976

March   After receipt of appointment – 17 March appoint Chaplain by Letter. Arrange swearing in of Under Sheriffs (3)

April   1 April – Take over. 6 April Judges's one day visit – Lunched with him in the Shirehall. 9 April – attend reception RAF Hereford. 14 April – Lunch together with Lord Lieutenant with Officers of the Worcestershire Regiment at Norton Barracks. 15 April – meet the Queen and the Duke of Edinburgh at Hereford Station, and with them to the Maundy Service in Hereford Cathedral. Consider nominations For roll of Sheriffs due to be submitted in May.

May   20 May – Attend opening service of Festival 1976 at Hereford Cathedral – lunch with the Bishop of Hereford. 25 May – lunch At Police Headquarters Hindlip with Chief Constable. And Dine as Guest of Honour aboard HMS *Antrim* (Missile Destroyer) in Avonmouth Docks. 27 May – Lunch with the Mayor of Hereford – Mayor making ceremony.

June   9 June – Mayor's Dinner at Worcester. 15 June – meet Princess Anne for Three Counties Show at Malvern. 25 June – Regimental Garden Party at Norton Barracks. 26 June – Festival Garden Party at Hereford.

July   3 July – Open Church Fete at Bushley as High Sheriff. 27
                July – attend Royal Garden Party at Buckingham Palace.

August   21 August – Give tea party to the Three Choirs at Hereford
                and afterwards receive the guests at an evening reception
                together with the Bishop and Sir Peter Scarlett. 22 August
                – Lunch with the Mayor of Hereford and parade with the
                Corporation and Band as High Sheriff of the City through
                the streets to the Opening Service in the Cathedral. 23
                August – attend the Three Choirs Supper and Reception. 26
                August – attend the Three Choirs concert in the Cathedral
                and the reception afterwards in the Shirehall at Hereford.

September

October   3 October – Welcome the Judge. 4 October – Judicial
                service in Worcester Cathedral – sit in Court with the Judge
                and lunch with the Chaplain and Under-Sheriff. 5 October
                – in Court and lunch with the Chaplin and Under-Sheriff.
                6 October – sit in Court and give High Sheriff's Luncheon
                in the Guildhall at Worcester. 7 October – sit in Court and
                lunch with the Chaplain and Under-Sheriff. Court closes.
                Judge comes to dine with the the High Sheriff. 9 October
                – Stand in for the Lord Lieutenant to represent the Queen
                at the Grand Priory of the Order of St John Service in
                Hereford Cathedral. 16 October – Attend the Mayor's
                Reception at the Guildhall in Worcester. 24 October as
                High Sheriff invited to read the Lesson in Tewkesbury
                Abbey at the Appeal Thanksgiving Service.

November   14 November – Armistice Service in Worcester Cathedral.
                16 November Guest of Honour at Herefordshire Law
                Society Dinner in Hereford.

December

1977
January   11 January – Attend the Lord Lieutenant's (Admiral Sir
                Deric Holland-Martin) Funeral. 21 January attend Admiral
                Sir Deric Holland-Martin's Memorial Service at Worcester
                Cathedral. 28 January attend the final Regimental Mess

Party at Norton Barracks Worcester. 31 January Monday –
Welcome the High Court Judge.

February 1 February Tuesday – Attend the Judicial Service in
Worcester Cathedral and the Court – lunch with the
Chaplain and Under-Sheriff. 2 February Wednesday –
Attend Court. 3 February Thursday – Attend Court and
thereafter give Judge's Dinner at Home. 4 February Friday
– Attend Court. 15 February Tuesday – Dine with the High
Court Judge at Shirehall in Worcester.

March 6 March Saturday – Dine with the Bishop of Worcester at
Hartlebury Castle. 26 March Saturday – Lunch with the Earl
and Countess Beauchamp at Madresfield Court.

April 1 April – Hand over to the new High Sheriff in the
Under-Sheriff's Office in Worcester and give them lunch in
the Union Club.

HIGH SHERIFF'S DIARY 1976/7

A TRANSCRIPT OF THE APPOINTMENT OF HIGH SHERIFF

SEAL OF THE
PRIVY COUNCIL

AT THE COURT AT BUCKINGHAM PALACE
The 17th Day of March 1976

PRESENT
THE QUEEN'S MOST EXCELLENT MAJESTY IN COUNCIL

To David Vernon Swynfen Cottrell Esquire
Of Rectory Farm Cottage
Kemerton
Tewkesbury

WHEREAS HER MAJESTY was this day pleased, by and with the
advice of HER PRIVY COUNCIL, to nominate you for, and appoint
you to be HIGH SHERIFF of the County of HEREFORD AND
WORCESTER during HER MAJESTY'S PLEASURE: These are
therefore to require you to take the Custody and Charge of the said

COUNTY, and duly to perform the duties of HIGH SHERIFF thereof during HER MAJESTY'S PLEASURE, whereof you are duly to answer according to Law.

Dated this 17th day of March 1976
    BY HER MAJESTY'S COMMAND
      N.E. LEIGH

Notes:

Although the appointment is made during March the duties change over on the 1st April.

It is also interesting to note that my Friend Admiral Sir Deric Holland-Martin GCB DSO DSC, who lived in my village of Kemerton, was at almost the same time appointed Her Majesty's Lieutenant for the County of Hereford and Worcester.

Diary entries

Tuesday 23 March 1976

I had great pleasure in calling upon the Rector of Kemerton, the Reverend Francis Moss, to formally appoint him as Chaplain, and received his letter of assent.

I then went over to Worcester to attend the Swearing In of the three Under-Sheriffs.

Tuesday 6 April 1976

The 1st Judge's visit

I collected the Chaplain (The Rev F.D. Moss MA – Rector of Kemerton) at about 9 a.m., and we motored over to Worcester, where we met the Under-Sheriff (Charles Whateley) at the Judge's Lodging in the Shirehall at around 10 a.m. We then proceeded up the Grand Staircase to meet the Judge Mr Justice May and to have a short chat with him.

The Court opened at 10.30 a.m., and we were to witness the sentencing of a number of men who had pleaded guilty to varying offences. This was to be a one-day sitting only for this specific purpose. The first case is worth mentioning. An Irishman, who had been settled in Hereford for a long time with his family, was, as the evidence showed, normally a well behaved chap.

He was in Hereford Market one day and went into a local inn afterwards. He met there one of the cattle dealers who had had too much to drink, and who was being a general nuisance. The defendant Irishman told this man to go away, whereupon the man turned on him and called him 'an Irish pig'. The accused Irishman then hit the man, or more nearly shoved him, whereupon the man fell, and hit his head on the quarry tile floor of the bar, and later died in hospital. The Judge found that a charge of manslaughter was justified, but after conferring with me (sitting as is customary beside him as a County Magistrate for the year) he bound the accused over for two years with a suspended sentence, and at the same time released him as a victim of misfortune.

It might in my opinion have happened to anyone, a case of justice with mercy.

When we had arrived in the morning, we had been asked to lunch with the Judge in his lodging, and so my wife Marylena joined the Chaplain, Under-Sheriff, and myself for lunch with the Judge. Charles Whateley (who this year was completing 50 years as an Under-Sheriff) told me that this was the first time that a High Sheriff had lunched with a Judge during a sitting, so we felt greatly honoured. I must say that we very much enjoyed the company of this very pleasant Judge, and we had a most excellent lunch.

In the afternoon we dealt with a number of other sentences. The Court rose soon after five, and we said goodbye and took our leave.

Friday 9 April 1976
Reception at RAF Hereford
This reception was given by Group Captain J.L. Clayson and his Officers.

We were looked after by Squadron Leader Youdan, who introduced us to a number of Herefordshire locals. Apart from this we met John Easthaugh, the Bishop of Hereford, and his wife Bridget (Daughter of Sir Hugh Chance) – very old friends of ours. We also met Superintendent Painter, who was to be responsible for Police supervision for the forthcoming Royal Visit in Hereford, and told us the best route to take in to the railway station to meet the Royal Train the next week.

Wednesday 14 April 1976
Worcestershire Regimental Lunch
I was invited to lunch with the Officers of the Worcestershire Regiment at Norton Barracks Worcester. I arrived at about 12.45 p.m. to see Sir

Deric Holland-Martin on the steps of the Officers' Mess, and we were both received by Colonel Bowen. It was an entertaining lunch (and as I later found out probably the last of such functions, as the Barracks were to close soon after the end of the year).

Amongst those Officers present were my friends Colonel Roy Harrison, Major Jack Somers, Brigadier Donald Knott, and Colonel John Ricketts. Colonel Bill Bowen the present Colonel of the Regiment presided.

Thursday 15 April 1976
The Queen's visit to Hereford
It was cold when we left this morning for Hereford, though the weather forecast was more promising. We arrived as advised by Superintendent Painter in view of the crowds. We were shown in to the Station Manager's office in Hereford Station at 10.15 a.m. where we were kindly supplied with a warming cup of coffee. Here we met up with many of the party for the presentation and welcome. These included the following: the Lord Lieutenant Admiral Sir Deric Holland-Martin and Lady Rosamund Holland-Martin — looking superb, the Chief Constable Mr A.A. Rennie and his wife, Colin Sheppard MP for Hereford and his wife, the Chairman of the County Council Sir Michael Higgs and Lady Higgs, the Mayor of Hereford Councillor M.K. Prendergast, and others.

After the coffee we were ushered onto the red carpet on the platform, where most delightfully we were placed next to the Holland-Martins at the head of the queue. Then ensued some amusing small talk, and the sun started to shine upon us. There was the Admiral in his full uniform and medals, standing next to an Able Seaman in morning dress with medals, to greet the Sovereign. My mind went back to my week in the company of an Admiral in Iceland when serving in HMS *Kent*. A minute or two later in came the Royal Train, which was quite magnificent with its two blue engines at the head, and a line of deep maroon coaches behind.

Presently out stepped the Queen and Prince Philip to be greeted by the Lord Lieutenant. They looked superb and seemingly ageless. The moment of a lifetime to some of us, when it happens you hardly can believe it. The Duke, who had evidently been briefed, remarked as he shook my hand that it seemed to be quite a Naval occasion. It is hard to record anything other than joy about such an occasion, and one's natural nervousness seems to evaporate as it happens. Our lovely Queen seems to have such charm, which was so overwhelming when subsequently She distributed the Maundy money in the Cathedral.

We were driven behind the Queen in a Limousine which also conveyed the Clerk of the County Council Mr Rennie and his wife, and also Sir Michael and Lady Higgs. The Service was memorable, and would have been all the more so had we not been so privileged as to have been present at the same service in Tewkesbury Abbey a year or two before.

The drive through the streets, which were crowded with loyal subjects all the way to the Cathedral, had been an interesting experience. There is no doubt about the exceptional interest of people in this part of our country in the monarchy. After the service there was a reception given by the Dean, followed by lunch in the Town Hall given by the Mayor. It had been a great occasion.

Thursday 20 May 1976

The opening service of festival 1976 at Hereford

We arrived at the Cathedral in Hereford at 10.30 a.m. I went into the Public Library, opposite the west door of the Cathedral, to find the robing room, where the two Lords Lieutenants Admiral Sir Deric Holland-Martin, and Colonel Dugdale (Shropshire, which is in part of the Hereford Diocese), and the two High Sheriffs Colonel Armistead and myself along with Mr John Cotterell, the Vice Chairman of the County Council were all to assemble. My wife had gone ahead direct into the Cathedral to take up her seat.

In the robing room was the Lord Lieutenant of Shropshire bending over a chair, as if to be caned, with his wife struggling to put his spurs on, a matter which was causing some amusement. At about 10.50 a.m. Colonel Armistead and I assembled in the hall of the Library to head the procession into the Cathedral. We were anxiously waiting for Mr Alan Hing, the Under-Sheriff, for Herefordshire, whose duty it was to proceed in front of us with his Staff of Office. We could see the Dean and Chapter at the west door of the Cathedral anxiously looking at their watches as it was one minute to go by then. Just as we had decided to leave on our own, I saw Mr Hing, with his Staff at the trail arms position, running towards us across the churchyard, so we stopped for him. He immediately fell in in front of us, and our procession hastened to the west door, with the two Lords Lieutenants bringing up the rear.

Tuesday 25th May 1976
Lunch at the West Mercia Police Headquarters
This was a day of lovely weather. At 12.30 p.m. we arrived for lunch with Mr A.A. Rennie the Chief Constable of West Mercia Police at their headquarters at Hindlip Hall near Worcester. We were introduced to all the senior Officers and their wives. We also met again the High Sheriff of Shropshire Colonel Armistead and his wife, as of course the policing area of West Mercia includes Shropshire, so it was nice to renew our aquaintance with them.

We had a very good lunch with the Chief Constable, and then toured the Control room which was full of electronic gadgets. Also we toured the Police training college at Droitwich, which I found most impressive. They had a television theatre where they could enact various situations in a mock up of a Police Station for training purposes. The training was thorough and so those passing out knew their job, like we did in the Royal Navy.

We had tea at the Training College, and then we returned back home to change, myself into my Royal Yacht Squadron mess kit, to proceed to Avonmouth to dine aboard HMS *Antrim*.

Tuesday 25 May 1976 p.m.
Dinner aboard HMS *Antrim*
Having been driven down to Avonmouth Docks in a taxi, because not only were we having a long day, but I knew about the exceptional quality of Naval hospitality, we boarded HMS *Antrim* at precisely 7.45 p.m., and received a very friendly welcome from Captain R.M.Burgoyne RN and his Officers. After drinks were served we had an excellent dinner, and indeed drank the Queen's health over the port sitting down, in the well known Naval tradition.

After dinner we were shown up to the bridge, which was surprisingly small for a ship of some 5000 tons, HMS *Antrim* being a guided missile Destroyer, so called, as she was more the size of a Second World War light Cruiser. We then went down in the Captain's lift to the Control Room; this took some time as there were about 16 of us in the party. We were introduced to Mr Lloyd Robinson and his wife, a well known local from Bristol. We were also introduced to Admiral Beresford-Pearce and his wife, who turned out to be great friends of a Naval friend of mine who served with the Admiral.

The High Sheriff of Avon and his wife, and some of the other surrounding High Sheriffs from Somerset, Gloucestershire, and Glamorgan were there also. Admiral Beresford-Pearce fortunately told me that none of the other guests could leave the party before I did as the senior High Sheriff present, and therefore the Guest of Honour. I should have realized that my wife and I were seated on the right of our hosts at the dinner, silly me! We then immediately took our leave at 12.25 a.m. having thanked our splendid Naval hosts, having had a memorable and long day.

Footnote:

1. Apparently, so I learned from this occasion, because of its loyalty during the Civil War Charles II not only granted the City of Worcester its magnificent Guildhall, which I had been aware of, but according to the Navy promoted its Sheriff to be the most senior.
2. HMS *Antrim* was subsequently to figure prominently in the Falkland Islands Campaign of 1982. Indeed the surrender of the Argentinian forces on South Georgia was taken on board her. Though by then she was under a different Captain.

Thursday 27 May 1976
Installation of the 595th Mayor of Hereford
We arrived at 10.45 a.m. at Hereford Town Hall for the Mayor Making ceremony. I sat next to the Dean of Hereford and managed to arrange with him the possibility that we might persuade the Circuit Judge to attend a service in the Cathedral at 10.30 a.m. on October 10. So now all is clear to get the Under-Sheriffs to persuade the Circuit Administrator to put up a case to the Judge for the ceremony to be held at Hereford.

Returning to the Mayor's Installation, this was clearly a quaint and traditional ceremony of great interest to us who had never seen one. The new Mayor Councillor W.A. Vowles BA made a very brief and witty speech (He was a Schoolmaster, and a Liberal Mayor). I liked his reference to the fact that the Dail had suggested that to conform to the continental standards, cars should drive on the right of the road in the Irish Republic, and if it was a success then this could be applied to lorries at a later date!

After the ceremony we went down to the reception where we were well received by the previous Mayor Councillor M.K. Prendergast (a Labour Mayor), and the Town Clerk. I found that the Hereford

Authorities were most enthusiastic about the prospect of us trying to engineer a visit by the Crown Court Judge in this Vintage year. A character by the name of Captain Kidd described the various treasures of the exceptional City Plate to us, Captain Kidd being the Mayor's Officer. It really was superb, there were some lovely 17th century pieces set in a beautiful floral setting in the assembly hall. My wife and I were very much absorbed in this when we met the Bishop and his wife, and Mrs Sheppard the wife of the Hereford MP. We then met the Mayor's Chaplain the Rev Burgoyne, a charming man, and various other interesting people to talk to. We left having signed the Visitors' Book at 2.45 p.m.

Footnote:

Whilst serving the Crown I had been ordered to drop all forms of Political allegiance or discussion for my year in office. This was great, because as mentioned above the two Mayors were of different parties, and we all became friendly as people serving the Crown and not politics.

Tuesday 15 June 1976

Visit of Princess Anne to the Three Counties Show

This was a dry day like most others in this year of drought. However it was fortunately not too hot. We were to be picked up by a police car, and were to be driven in front of another police car containing the Lord Lieutenant and Lady Holland-Martin. (Somewhat uniquely both of us Queen's Representatives in the County live in the same village of Kemerton so we went on this occasion in convoy.) We were driven through Worcester, where we were escorted by two police outriders on motorcycles, and the traffic had been stopped for us to pass through without hindrance. Another escort met us outside Malvern, and the streets of Malvern were cleared also to allow us through unhindered, altogether the journey there and back was well organized.

We were taken direct to the Abbey School playing fields where with the Holland-Martins and the Chief Constable we met Princess Anne in the Helicopter of the Queen's Flight of the RAF. She then toured the Show with us, and opened it officially. At lunch time she was presented to the guests, and presided over the official lunch with a short speech. Later on in the afternoon we went to see her off, in the very large twin-engined helicopter, and waved her goodbye. It had been a very pleasant day and the Princess was in good form.

Friday 25 June 1976
Regimental Cocktail Party
This was I believe the last party to be held at Norton Barracks before it was closed, and fortunately it was a splendid summer's evening with the Band of the Regiment playing to us on the lawn. I met the Officers of the Regiment once again, and was introduced to their illustrious General ' Windy' Gale, who was for some years the Commander in Chief of the Rhine Army. Colonel Bowen, my host, had agreed earlier in the year to accept my nomination to the Sovereign that he should be placed on the list for selection of the future High Sheriffs, which I thought appropriate in view of the departure of the Regiment from Worcester, which was sad for us in the County.

Saturday 26 June 1976
Festival Garden Party – Hereford
We both attended a very pleasant Garden Party as part of the ongoing Festival celebrations, the Mayor and the other usual dignitaries being present.

Tuesday 29 June 1976
Dinner at Trinity College Cambridge
This dinner had nothing to do with the High Sheriff's Year, but as it happened within my year of Office, which had been recorded amongst the list of distinctions gained by members of the College, and as such an invitation only occurs at my age (53) every seven years, I have thought it worthy of a mention at this time.

I arrived in Cambridge in the late afternoon and having found my rooms, went through to look at the lovely Backs forming the frontage to the River Cam. I did not meet anyone that I knew until about 7.30 p.m., when I went over to Neville's Court for a drink before the dinner. Almost immediately I saw the familiar face of Mark Ward, a good friend and an Harrovian doctor, inimitable as ever, it seemed almost that we had never left the place some thirty five years before! Following upon him I saw Euan Montgomerie who had already reserved our places in the Dining Hall. I also saw Humphrey Evans and Carly Tufnell on the way into Hall.

I will leave the reader of this, if there is ever one, to guess whether the liquor or the very good dinner was best! At least they put us up in College for the night, and give us a good breakfast before we left in the morning.

Saturday 3 July 1976
Opening the church fete at Bushley
This must have been one of England's hottest days through this particular summer, which was one of the finest on record anyway. I had been invited as the High Sheriff to make an opening speech, which in the event I cut down to about three sentences of encouragement. This was in order to save everyone from standing about on the most amazingly hot day you could imagine in this country.

Tuesday 27 July 1976
Royal Garden Party at Buckingham Palace
Fortunately this was a beautiful day as ever during this ever dry summer. We parked in the Mall at about 3 p.m., and strangely enough, next to us was John Wells MP (Maidstone) and his wife Lucinda. She was a Meath-Baker of Hasfield Court near Gloucester, and I was in my free days one of her admirers. I introduced my wife Marylena, and we together walked along the Mall and through the front gates on into the Palace Courtyard, where we had to give our invitations up. We proceeded up through the Palace, and out into the Garden on the other side. Tea was in a Marquee, and a band was playing on the lawn.

The Queen and Prince Philip came out and walked around talking to the guests. We saw a number of other people we knew there, including Riddian Vaughan who was an Officer in the Guards by then, Colonel Bowen, and strangely enough the O'Connors, who used to have a house at Yarmouth, Isle of Wight, and whom I had not seen for years. Patrick O'Connor, in whose Y class yacht I used to sail occasionally, was now a High Court Judge.

We had a long walk around the Gardens, which were lovely, with a lake in the middle. This was an epic and interesting afternoon, and it was fun to see inside part of the lower floors of the Palace.

Saturday 21 August 1976
High Sheriff's Tea Party at Hereford
This year being Hereford's Centenary Year the Three Choirs Festival was at Hereford Cathedral. During the beginning of the Festival it is usual for the High Sheriff to give a tea party for the Three Choirs taking part, and it was my pleasure to preside over such a party in the Cloisters. This was an enjoyable occasion on yet another fine afternoon, and it was

fun to meet members of the Choirs and the Conductor Roy Massey, the Master of Music at Hereford.

The Three Choirs Festival Reception
Later that evening I was requested to receive along with the Bishop of Hereford John Easthaugh and Sir Peter Scarlett, the Chairman of the Three Choirs Festival, some hundred or more distinguished guests, including many Americans, who had been invited to a drink at the Bishop's magnificent Palace next door to the Cathedral. One American could not account for the fact that I neither had a fancy hat, nor a gun!

Sunday 22 August 1976
Festival Parade around Hereford
As I was due to walk around the City of Hereford just ahead of the Mayor, between him and the Aldermen, I was very pleased that we had yet another dry and sunny day. We set off from the Town Hall at 10.30 a.m., with a band at the head of the procession, followed by the Councillors and Aldermen in their robes followed by the Deputy Mayor (who was the Mayor at the time of the Royal Visit) who was a History Master, and a labour member of the Council. He was most kind and gave me a run-down on the history of many city buildings as we marched. The Mace Bearer preceded the Mayor of course. I was dressed in a morning coat with black waistcoat and black silk hat also wearing medals. We were an entertaining sight no doubt!

Perhaps I should mention that I was the first High Sheriff since the Local Government reorganization two years previously to have been invited to march in this procession as High Sheriff of the City of Hereford. Previously there had been two High Sheriffs of each separate County, and also a Sheriff of Worcester city and the city of Hereford. My two predecessors in office and I had now to carry out all of these functions, when so required as an amalgamation of four people as it were at our own extra expense.

We finally marched our way into the Cathedral through the west door to be greeted by a fanfare, and the start of the Festival Service for the commencement of the Three Choirs Festival, which was most enjoyable. After the Service we had a splendid lunch in the Town Hall.

Monday 23 August 1976
The Three Choirs Supper and Reception by the Bishop

This was a very jolly supper party given by our friends the Easthaughs on a lovely evening by the River Wye, which was most enjoyable.

Thursday 26 August 1976
Festival and Reception at the Shirehall
We were privileged to be asked to attend a performance by the Three Choirs in the Cathedral, and then go on to a supper given by them in the Shirehall at Hereford. This was a rather pleasant building and we had a most enjoyable time there. This was the end of quite a busy week in Hereford, which we both had enjoyed throughout.

Sunday 3 October 1976
Welcome for the Circuit Judge
At 5.55 p.m. we arrived at the Shirehall Worcester, where I met the Under-Sheriff (Charles Whateley), and within a few minutes we were ushered into the presence of the Judge Mr Justice Talbot and Lady Talbot. We had a very pleasant and relaxed conversation with them for about three quarters of an hour over a glass of sherry, and then took our leave of them.

Monday 4 October 1976
Judge's Visit and Judicial Service
Having collected the Chaplain (Rev F.D. Moss) we arrived at the Shirehall Sheriff's Room at 9.45 a.m., and later on we were ushered into the Judge's presence in the upstairs drawing room by his Marshal. After some conversation the Chaplain and I joined the Judge in his car, which had a Union Flag flying on the bonnet. We arrived in no time at the Cathedral with a police escort, because the main street in Worcester had been closed to traffic, and there were policemen on every road junction.

At 10.30 a.m. on arrival we processed into the Cathedral for the usual Judicial Service of Matins. The Choir was provided by the Boys of the King's School in the Cathedral Close, and apart from the Anthems their rendering of Psalm 101 was memorable. I suppose that the Service lasted for some forty minutes, after which the Judge took his leave of the Dean, and we were driven once again in state back to the Shirehall. Whereupon we all processed through the Judge's Lodging into the Court where the warrant of assize was read to a fairly full Court.

The Judge first of all dealt with a case of attempted murder, which he sent back for a further medical report. Then he dealt with another case of the same sort which involved a mistress who was the accused's brother's wife! But in this case there appeared to be extenuating circumstances involving a suicide pact. The next case was in connection with an armed robbery of a village Post Office near Stourport. It was a particularly distressing case of a villain holding up two women while he robbed the place, putting them in fear of their lives, and although he pleaded guilty he was rightly given 5 years for his efforts.

The third case for trial was supposed to last for several days, and concerned an Indian man on a charge of Murder, the leading Counsel involved were Mr Stuart Shields QC and Mr Pratam Singh QC. There was a tremendous business of selecting a jury mostly of women. I cannot think that this case was particularly interesting, and it in fact collapsed by the end of the first day due to lack of evidence. That was on the Tuesday evening.

Wednesday 6 October 1976
The High Sheriff's Lunch in the Guildhall, Worcester
The trial mentioned above had collapsed by this morning, and as I had my luncheon that day already planned, I went off with the Under-Sheriff and Chaplain to get a good bottle of port for the Judge, who was due to dine with us later in the week. We went into Smithy's and duly purchased the port, whereupon he offered us a tour of the maze of cellars there, and also a sherry tasting session.

Needless to say we enjoyed ourselves so much, that when we surfaced and strolled round to the Guildhall we were only just in time for the line up for the luncheon guests, who included the lawyers from the Courts, which is the prime purpose of a High Sheriff's lunch by tradition. We received many comments of appreciation from the guests afterwards. Needless to say I was very grateful to the Mayor for the use of the Guildhall and to my dear wife for organizing it all.

Thursday 7 October 1976
End of the Judge's Visit
As there was no court sitting today, and I had already offered the Under-Sheriff and Chaplain a lunch in the Union Club, we kept this appointment at lunchtime, and went into Worcester for lunch. That evening the Judge came with his wife and dined with us at home, and we had a number of friends in to meet them, making up a party of eight.

Saturday 9 October 1976
National Order of St John Service of Re-dedication
Because Admiral Sir Deric Holland-Martin was unable to attend and represent the Queen at this service, I was commanded by the Queen to represent her at this great occasion for the Order. It was attended by members of the Order from all over the British Isles. I had briefed the Under-Sheriff of the Herefordshire Bailiwick, Alan Hing, so that he would be very promptly on time at the west door of the Cathedral to meet us and lead us in. Having had lunch at the Hereford Police Headquarters, the members of the order, or rather the big noises of the order like Lord Caccia, the Lord Prior, departed to the Cathedral, to robe and prepare for their procession. We then got into a police car and were driven round the city, and then arrived in front of the west door of the Cathedral at precisely the appointed time of 1.58 p.m. to be greeted by the Under-Sheriff with his Staff of Office, dead on time. My wife and I proceeded in procession behind the Under-Sheriff to the west door of the Cathedral, which we had been briefed would then open to a fanfare of trumpets.

When we got to the west door nothing happened, so I suggested to Alan Hing that he should knock on the door three times with the base of his Staff like a prelate, much to the merriment of the press and crowd standing nearby! This he did, only to have the door opened slightly by a Verger, who apologized for the delay, and said that they were not ready for us yet, and shut the door! We stood there for about 2 minutes in a shocked sense of amusement, which we shared with the crowd, and which made the job seem easy thereafter. Then suddenly the doors opened and a great fanfare of trumpets rang out and we processed up in accordance with the precedent with my wife slightly behind (for the only time!) up to the two thrones on the left hand side under the tower, and facing the Lord Prior.

This was a great Service, leaving aside one's own role in it, because of course the robes of the Order and the pageantry were magnificent, and the hymns appropriate to the occasion. Imagine finding yourself sitting on a throne, like we did, with Bishops, Lord Priors and others bowing to you! You feel that it is a bit unreal, if you are not used to it, though at the same time one had a strange feeling that it was all part of the ordinary life that by now one was getting used to. Was this therefore the greatest moment during the year of office? No I think not – some of the real rather than symbolic moments were more memorable.

We had tea in the Shirehall after the Service, where amongst others we met our longstanding friends Commander Edwin Morrison RN (Retd) and his wife Valerie. Edwin is a fellow member of the Royal Yacht Squadron, and I have several times sailed with him at Cowes. He is one of the Knights of the Order, and high up in the Hierarchy, and they had come up from Hampshire for the occasion. There were many local people there like Sir Hugo Huntingdon-Whiteley and his wife Jenny, who is one of the Chiefs of the Order in Worcestershire. Any way it was an interesting and unusual day for us, which strangely enough we managed to enjoy and take in our stride.

Saturday 16 October 1976
The Mayor of Worcester's Reception
This was held in the Magnificent Guildhall at Worcester, in the Mayor's Parlour, and was a small drinks party for the City fathers, Dean, Bishop, and so on. As the High Sheriff, since re-organization in 1974, is now Sheriff of the city, as well as the county, as in the case of Hereford City, we rank amongst the city dignitaries, and we get invited to these pleasant occasions.

Sunday 24 October 1976
Dedication Festival at Tewkesbury Abbey
Canon Pouncey, the Vicar of Tewkesbury, in view of me being a Trustee of the Tewkesbury Abbey appeal, asked me to read the Lesson at this Festival Service in my capacity of High Sheriff which was published. My wife, it is interesting to record, had raised by an auction sale, for which she was Chairman of the Committee, the magnificent sum of £20,000, and more eventually.

Thursday 28 October 1976
HMS *Ganges* closes
I Entered HMS *Ganges* as a volunteer recruited at Cambridge in early 1942. As I have previously recorded, I did three months basic training there as an Ordinary Seaman paid at 1s 6d per day. This included climbing the famous mast there. It so happens that this great training ship, which was considered one of the best for training Ratings was closed in this particular year, due to defence cuts, and I have felt it worth recording in view of the personal connection with my past.

Sunday 14 November 1976

The Remembrance Service at Worcester Cathedral

The weather on this occasion was quite dreadful, there was freezing fog, even when we processed to the War Memorial outside the Cathedral after the Service. I am glad to say that both our daughters and their husbands were able to accompany us to this solemn and formal occasion, and to the reception given by the Dean afterwards. This is the one occasion when all the Deputy Lieutenants turn out in their rows as well.

Admiral Sir Deric Holland-Martin looked very frail in the extreme cold. He was sitting next to me, and just as the Service was about to begin his copious medals started to slip out of their fastening, and I had to help him by holding them as he re-secured them. The medals were certainly an unexpected weight! He and I, at the end of the Service in the Cathedral, processed out behind the Deputy Lieutenants to attend the wreath-laying by the Legion and Armed Services on the Cathedral Green. As I have already related it was still freezing out there, and it did none of us any good, and least of all the Admiral who did not seem at all well due to the conditions. What a pity that we cannot have this important occasion transferred to the Battle of Britain Day in September when the weather is warm, since that was the deciding battle of the Second World War, though as a Naval man I may be taken to task for admitting it, and there are few of the 1918 Armistice left. We might then prolong the lives of us later Veterans. That very sadly was the last time I saw my good Friend the Admiral.

Tuesday 16 November 1976

Herefordshire Law Society Dinner

I had the honour to be invited to attend the Annual Dinner of the Herefordshire, Breconshire, and Radnorshire Incorporated Law Society. I arrived at 7.15 p.m. outside the Green Dragon Hotel, and to my surprise I found a parking space opposite. It had been an easy drive over on a fine warm evening in contrast to the weather two days earlier. I entered and introduced myself to an obvious official wearing a pendant, whom I correctly took to be the President. In the next half hour I was introduced to, or variously met, The Mayor, Councillor Vowles; Superintendant Painter; Captain Kidd in his usual jovial form; The Bishop of Shrewsbury; The Recorder Gordon Slinn QC; The Dean of Hereford; The Local President of the British Medical Association; and also the President of the local Chartered Accountants Association. We as the top table guests were clapped in and out, as is the custom apparently. I was the guest of honour sitting on the President's right-hand side. The best speeches came from the Dean and the Bishop, it was their evening. One of the Bishop's stories went down very well with the assembled company. A Judge seeing an accused man in the dock apparently undefended asked him if he wished to have a Defence Counsel. Whereupon the accused man said that his defence rested with God. The Judge then remarked that this was a very proper thought. However said the Judge, I consider your interests would at the moment be better served if you were to instruct someone to defend you who is a little nearer to this Locality.

It was a great evening, and it was very nice to be amongst one of our richest of all professions again, most enjoyable. After a drink (soft!) in the ante-room, I took my leave of the President Mr Price, at the same time as the Bishop, at about midnight, and then drove home, arriving back at about 1 a.m.

Friday 11 January 1977
Admiral Sir Deric Holland-Martin's Funeral
The saddest thing about my Year in Office was to lose the Admiral, who died on Thursday 6 January 1977. We had so enjoyed working together in the two respective Crown Offices, a pretty unique thing to find, as apart from already being friends, both these Offices were held, in a very large county, by residents in one village. All that I can say is that it was a great privilege to serve with such a distinguished man, in the last year of his life, and we shall always remember him.

The Memorial Service for Admiral Sir Deric Holland-Martin GCB DSO DSC was held in Worcester Cathedral on Friday 21 January 1977, presided over by both the Bishops of Worcester and Hereford, at which of course we were present.

Saturday 28 January 1977
Norton Barracks – The final party
As recorded previously this had been a year of finality for the Regiment, and we were invited to the final party given by Colonel Bowen, the Colonel of the Regiment. The Mess was full up with guests, and we all enjoyed this last fling, in spite of the underlying sadness of the event. On the bright side Barbara Dean, the widow of Colonel Dean, an Officer of

the Regiment, got engaged to Tony Morris a former Officer in the Territorials of the Regiment. So there was some happiness in an otherwise unhappy event.

Monday 31 January 1977
Visit of the Judge
As is customary Charles Whateley the Under-Sheriff and I attended on the Judge, Mr Justice May, at 6 p.m. this evening at the Lodgings, and took a glass of sherry with him to discuss the next day's events.

Tuesday 1 February 1977
Judicial service and court
At 9 a.m. I motored to the Rectory, and picked up my Chaplain (Reverend F.D. Moss), and having negotiated the icy roads on to the M5 Motorway, we proceeded along in my Range Rover to Worcester to arrive at the Judge's Lodging at the Shirehall at 9.45 a.m. We went up to meet the Judge at 10 a.m. precisely. The sun was out, and I am glad to say that it was a perfect crisp February day.

After being photographed, we got into two Limousines, the Judge being in the second one, flying the Union Flag on its bonnet, together with the Chaplain and myself. We arrived at the Cathedral at 10.30 a.m. to be greeted by the Dean (the Very Reverend T. Baker) and the Chapter, together with the Archdeacon of Worcester and Colonel Bowen, the Cathedral Administrator, and then we processed in.

It was an impressive little procession with the Judge in his scarlet robes and full bottomed wig at the end of it. Thereupon followed morning matins with the most memorable singing by the Choir of the King's School (a public school) who gave a very fine rendering of Psalm 101, and an Anthem by Mozart. My wife much appreciated the Service as well as me.

After the Service we got back into our cars, after taking our leave of the Dean, and thanking him for the fine Service. We were whisked through the city by a police escort, which cleared the traffic, and as previously we processed straight through the Judge's Lodging into Court.

This was to be a Civil Court sitting, and the first case involved the conversion of a car for a disabled driver. The Plaintiff was an elderly man in a wheelchair, who had had both legs amputated. He gave his evidence, and was cross-examined together with the witnesses for his case prior to the luncheon adjournment.

When the Luncheon Adjournment was announced by the Judge, we processed out, and the Judge extended to us the very unusual, if not unique, privilege of being included in the High Sheriff's official photograph along with his Marshal. The photograph was a special one as it was the end of 50 years in Office of the Under-Sheriff, Charles Whateley.

The remainder of the day until 5.05 p.m. was taken up with the hearing of the case that we had heard in the morning. The disabled man won, I am glad to say, his case against the Garage, who had to pay him £700 Damages plus costs.

We said goodnight to the Judge after the case had ended, and the Chaplain and I drove home at 5.15 p.m.

Wednesday 2 February 1977
The second day in court
The Chaplain and I arrived at the Judge's Lodging at about 10 a.m., and at 10.30 a.m. precisely we processed into Court with the Judge. A new case then opened with three Queen's Counsel appearing. Mr Draycott QC. was for the Plaintiff, a bulldozer driver who had lost an arm in an accident, and who was suing both the transport lorry owners and also the owners of the machine for the damages incurred. Mr Walton QC appeared for the transporters.

The case that was outlined was that the bulldozer (or more technically named a Trackscavator) had been used for some ground levelling. It was being collected from the site one spring Saturday morning in 1973 by a low-loader lorry for transport to a cemetery. The bulldozer slipped off the lorry whilst being loaded, and also being driven by the Plaintiff. The question was, who was liable for the injury caused to the Plaintiff.

The trial was to last for two days so, except for the opening remarks by Counsel, we really only got through the Plaintiff's evidence during the first day. We went for lunch that day again to the Union and County Club, where we had the usual bottle of hock and some liver for lunch. I saw Brigadier Britten in the bar as well as the Club Hon Secretary Peter Seward, who happens to be my accountant.

Thursday 3 February 1977
The third day in court
The Court again assembled at 10.30 a.m., and we continued with the evidence of the driver of the low-loader. We heard evidence also from

a consulting engineer called in by the low-loader's owners. His evidence suggested that even though the bulldozer was loaded on a maximum 9 degree slope towards the side on which it slipped off, it would not have slipped off as a result of that slope, or any reasonable amount of oil or mud (which one might expect on the average low-loader). This was the state of the case as we adjourned for lunch across the road to the club again.

As we came out of Court the Judge asked me, as I was sitting with him as a County Magistrate of course, what I thought the cause of the accident might be. As we had heard from the bulldozer driver the day before that the machine had a tendency to hesitate on slewing, and we owned a similar machine in our marina at Tewkesbury, I suggested that from the evidence so far it would seem that the accident was caused by a fault on the machine. He said that he had also come to that conclusion.

In the afternoon the evidence of a fault on the hydraulic system, for which no evidence was brought to show that it had been corrected, was enough to clinch the case against the owners of the machine. The Judge's summing up was a masterpiece, which seemed to block any hope of some holes that the Defence lawyers might find to enable them to appeal. We then left as the Court adjourned early at the end of this case, and we arrived back at about 5 p.m.

That evening we were to have the Judge to dine, and the preparations by Mrs Crowther-Green and the Butler Mr Trussler were soon well in hand. Besides the Judge Sir John May and his Marshal, our Guests were Jean Vaughan (The widow of Lieutenant Colonel Peter Vaughan, who had he lived would have been the next but one High Sheriff), Major Stuart Howard and his wife Jose, and Ian and Katherine McPherson, who were with us by 7.30 p.m. The Judge arrived at about 8 p.m. The evening went reasonably well, the food excellently served, and the Taylor 1955 port being much appreciated.

Friday 4 February 1977
The fourth day in court
Again we got to the Court at 10 a.m. and processed in at 10.30 a.m. We had a new case today scheduled as a one day case. This case concerned a building contract for an incinerator used for smelting aluminium in Smethwick, somewhere near the M5 motorway. As this was to be our last day sitting in Court, and as the Judge had excused us from the

hearings of the second week, we left after lunch, and so I will not relate the few details that we heard. We had enjoyed this our last time in Court, and took our leave of the Judge and Under-Sheriff.

Tuesday 15 February 1977
Dinner with the Judge
We were invited to dine with Sir John and Lady May at the Judge's Lodging where we arrived at 7.45 p.m. sharp. While I was there I had to sign a paper authorizing the Chief Executive of the County Council to attend in my place a meeting with the Prince of Wales at Buckingham Palace on 23 February, to deal with the business relating to the Queen's Jubilee Appeal. (As the successor to Admiral Sir Deric Holland-Martin had not been appointed yet, in accordance with precedent I as High Sheriff had become Acting Lord Lieutenant as well). As I was signing this document in came Major and Mrs Hervey-Bathurst of Eastnor Castle, and we all went up to the Judge's drawing room, where we met the other guests. These were the Bishop of Worcester Robin Woods and his wife and David Annett, the Headmaster of the King's School at Worcester, and his wife, who were at the previous Judge's dinner party. We indeed had a most enjoyable evening. It turned out that the Judge's Marshal Christopher Vane was a Trinity Cambridge man. I suppose that one day his name might feature amongst the distinctions of the College as a Judge or a Law Officer of the Crown, an interesting supposition. There we are, a pleasant dinner party to end a memorable year, leaving aside the recent sadness.

Saturday 16 March 1977
Dinner at Hartlebury Castle
The Bishop of Worcester Robin Woods and his wife, who were friends of ours, very kindly asked us to dine with them, as part of our year in office, and a most enjoyable evening it was, the Bishop being on very good form. I discovered that he also was a Trinity Cambridge man.

Saturday 26 March 1977
Lunch at Madresfield Court with Earl Beauchamp
The last occasion of the year was to have lunch with Lord and Lady Beauchamp at Madresfield Court, where we admired the famous daffodils and the house and grounds. The Earl came in for lunch with his nurses, but he could not join in with the conversation very much due

to his failing health. However it was otherwise an enjoyable occasion, and to see Sir Hugo and Lady Huntingdon-Whiteley, Sir Hugo having been at school with me at Eton.

Here ends the High Sheriff's diary for 1976/7
I turned over the Office to Lieutenant Colonel E.C. (Teddy) Philips at the Under-Sheriff's Office in Worcester on 31 March 1977, the only ceremony in those days was to give the new incumbent and the Under-Sheriff lunch at the Union and County Club in Worcester. I had had to perform the office of Acting Lord Lieutenant for some three months during the vacancy, and as it turned out Colonel Philips had to do likewise, in fact I gather that he had a very busy time indeed during the summer months carrying out both Offices.

Appendix II

A lawyer's opinion about the need for law reforms in relation to property rights between neighbours, and also the reduction in costs in civil law cases

By now I am sure the reader understands that it was with reluctance that I became a solicitor rather than an Officer in the Royal Navy, or an engineer, or perhaps both. However, it was my inheritance, dating back for six generations of solicitors practising in Birmingham from father to son, which, as I have already related, when I qualified as the seventh was a record for the profession.

I decided to specialize in Company Law primarily as it was close to industry, and particularly the manufacturing industry, which interested me. However in those days when I first qualified in 1950, we all had to be GPS to start with,

Of course nowadays it is different and firms all have specialist Partners. I therefore viewed our Litigation department in an investigative manner, since I used to travel up by train for at least 45 minutes every day and could study some of their files. In many cases I ordered the advice given by the barristers to be overruled, and the matter to be settled out of Court to save the clients from incurring costs that they should be advised were not worth risking. However I will return to that subject later.

What really concerns me is that the Land Registration Acts, whilst giving a specific delineation of property and rights in relation to the planning, goes no further, and in consequence there are ongoing disputes between large numbers of neighbours which end up in the Courts. The Late Lord Denning, an outstanding Master of The Rolls, in his many judgements tried to get Parliament to address this situation without much success. What we really need is a codifying of the law between neighbouring properties, to prevent for instance the case of the woman who cut down a tree in her hedge, a matter which her neighbour disputed, which ended up in her going to prison, which I find very unacceptable.

Take my own case: the local Parish Council claimed a public right of way through part of my own and my neighbour's gardens, and I had to fight them for 21 years before we got justice. A Local Inquiry set up by the County Council, costing the ratepayers £25,000 in 1988, found that there was not a shred of evidence to their claim. I can well remember saying to the two solicitors representing the Ramblers Association and the Open Spaces Society, you have obviously lost your case, we are all solicitors, why do you not throw the towel in now, come and have lunch in the pub with me, and save everyone a lot of costs. Needless to say they declined because they had to justify their large accounts to their oversubscribed clients. The result was good to them, but apparently not their clients, as the Inspector and Minister found against them. Whilst I conducted our own and my neighbour's case against them, we were still left with some preliminary costs which the wretched Parish Council refused to refund, and which it was not worth the costs involved in my opinion to obtain against them. The Law totally fails in this respect, if people are assaulted as my neighbour and myself were over many years by continuing trespass, which should be punishable by community service as a crime, and anybody that is found to have been acting illegally should be made responsible for the damage done.

I have no time for the European Court of Human Rights as they take no account of our existing rights under Her Majesty The Queen, whose legal authority goes back over one thousand years. What we want in respect of land ownership is our own Code of Laws created by our own Parliament in relation to land ownership, just like the Romans had under the Emperor Justinian, something that I had to study in reading Law at Cambridge.

Unfortunately Parliament is overburdened by lawyers, and until we dis-enfranchise them like Clergymen, and send them to be, as they are now, represented in the House of Lords, we shall never get such reforms through, unless perhaps present restrictive practices are abandoned by the lawyers in general. The basic rights between neighbours could be set out in a book for all to read, and this alone would help neighbours, most of whom long to avoid disputes, and enable them to do just this. For example the Romans made provision for the maintenance of boundary hedges and walls. We do not even with the letter T inwards really regulate this in the same way that they did. For instance if you own a wall, particularly if the boundary is the wall of a dwellinghouse, does your neighbour have a right to grow for instance a Wisteria up against it? What about trees on a boundary, some are OK in the right place and of the right variety, but surely on a joint boundary there should be an agreement on species? Why not, as the Romans did on farmland, have a code that ownership should extend from one yard beyond a hedge or wall beyond the boundary, which would prevent the long running disputes as to who is responsible for what. I could go on for a long time as I feel that this particular branch of the law lets the country down.

The other aspect, which may be more important, is the subject of lawyer's costs, which has always troubled me, but far more so in the present day. On Tuesday 22 March 2005, I read in the *Daily Mail* of a woman, represented by a solicitor nicknamed ' JAWS', a divorce solicitor, who having lost her case for retaining the property in which she was dwelling as a separated partner, who continued to co-habit, got a lawyer's bill of £67,313. How totally disgraceful of my profession to allow such a bill to be charged. For what? The trouble is, and has been for years, that lawyers are allowed self regulating systems, the Bar Council and the Law Society, which seldom support the public in the case of costs being disputed. We need a regulatory system on which lawyers cannot sit.

Taking the matter further we need to stop the totally restrictive practices of lawyers as a whole. There is no need nowadays to have to employ up to three or more lawyers on a case in a Civil Court. This is entirely a restrictive practice, since anyway solicitors and barristers are trained together, and nowadays all lawyers specialize, so that the specialists of years ago are not required in the same way, as they are generally available. Other countries like Canada and New Zealand have firms of barristers and solicitors working together in one practice with one set of overhead costs. In this country now since in fact the 1930s, Judges have been able to be appointed from either barristers or solicitors, so that the idea of a separation between the two branches of these professions is no longer tenable, and they should be amalgamated to save the public unnecessary costs, otherwise in my view they are purely concerned in profiteering.

There is one more aspect to this subject, because if you look at the consistency of the House of Commons, you will see that lawyers outnumber the occupations of the rest of the House, and can therefore make sure that no change or reform in the law takes place in such a way that might damage their ability to ensure that the Civil Law system continues to support their generally over-charged costs. They in my opinion should therefore be disbarred from membership of that House, like clergymen, and be required to be represented in the House of Lords, though this would have to be enforced after an election.

Finally I do not think that the way the centralized system of the Crown Prosecution service works, it has distorted the system, as the preliminary hearing before Magistrates ensured the best possibility of local evidence coming forward. As a result of their bungling huge resources are wasted, this is witnessed in a trial reported on 31 March 2005 which failed, and which cost the tax payer £4,837,916 in barristers' fees, and £9,040,854 in solicitors' fees. How perfectly disgraceful, and all lawyers ought to be ashamed. However now I have made my point, and that is that. I do not suppose anything will be done about all this, as there are too many important people making their fortunes at it!

Index

Page numbers in italics indicate illustrations